Cinema in
Revolution

A Dziga Vertov poster for *Man with a Movie Camera*, 1929

CINEMA IN REVOLUTION

The Heroic Era of the Soviet Film

Edited by Luda and Jean Schnitzer
and Marcel Martin

Translated and with additional material
by David Robinson

HILL AND WANG   NEW YORK
A division of Farrar, Straus and Giroux

Contents

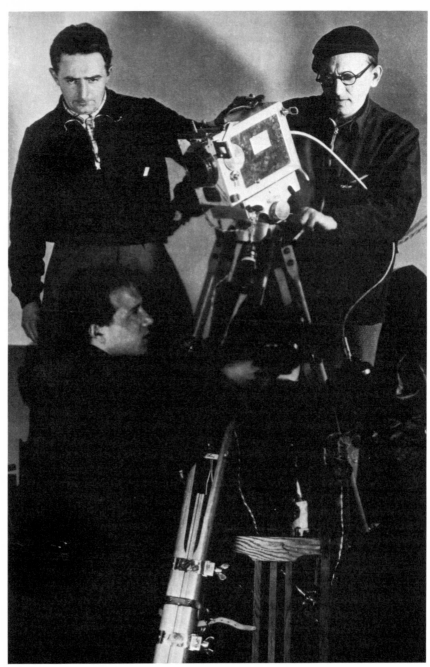

Dziga Vertov (top left) filming *Enthusiasm* (1931)

Introduction
by David Robinson

'They were astonishing and wonderful days,' writes Sergei Yuykevitch in the opening essay of this collection; 'the beginnings of a revolutionary art.' It is all too easy for us, in the West and in the 1970s, to forget the wonder. The brave youths of that time are old men now, if they have survived; and their films, if *they* have survived, have withered into classics, revered rather than seen, deteriorated into old, scratched prints, duped into a misty haze on film society screens.

But they *were* wonderful days. Perhaps there has never been and never will be quite such a boundless vision as opened before the young Soviet artists of the early 1920s. The past was dead and buried and (they vehemently said) rightly so. The future which was to prove so bitter for so many of this very generation was far off and unseen. But the present was all theirs; and they seized it eagerly. Kozintsev describes how three or four teenagers with enthusiasm as their only credential could be given a real theatre of their very own to play with. The world never more evidently belonged to the young: the only danger was that you might yet lose it to the still younger. Gerassimov amusingly describes how the leaders of the Theatre of the Eccentric Actor, having reached the mature age of twenty-two, found their positions threatened by a new avant-garde of sixteen years old who attacked their conservatism and academicism.

The arts of the past were all dead. The task was to build a new, a revolutionary, a socialist art – art that would serve the needs of an exciting, unprecedented, ideal new society. There were no rules, no precedents, no limits, no restrictions. It went without saying that the young were quite fearless. Why should they not have been? They had seen the apparently indestructible mass of the past disintegrate in a moment. Many of them had been combatants in the First World War, the Revolution, or the Civil War that followed. In this artistic free-for-all extravagance and eccentricity held the day: all that was necessary was energy and enthusiasm – and perhaps talent.

And it was astonishing what a forcing ground of talent the great new world of socialism proved to be. The boys who yelled Mayakovski songs about the streets of Kiev and Moscow and Petrograd, and painted buildings and banners, and improvised plays and performed puppet shows and argued and called meetings and argued some more, proved to be a generation as creatively gifted as any nation had known at any time; and their contribution to the arts of the twentieth century still deeply affects us today. Painting and the cinema seemed to be special beneficiaries: above all the Revolution gave the cinema Eisenstein, Pudovkin, Dovzhenko and Kuleshov, four masters who changed the entire course of cinema history.

In this book some of the youngsters of that enchanted generation, the founders of the Soviet cinema, recall the years and the exultation of their youth. Their essays do not add up to an exact and total history of the time, perhaps – indeed partialities and prejudices are very evident from time to time – but they do present a vivid picture of the atmosphere, the feeling, the excitement of a unique epoch; they do revive for us, half a century afterwards, the exaltation of those days.

In one special particular I think the publication of these essays gives a new aspect to the history of the early Soviet cinema. This is the extent of the influence upon the cinema of Vsevolod Emilievitch Meyerhold. Again and again his name recurs in the course of these essays, written quite independently of one another. Here, for the first time, it becomes abundantly clear that – apart from the climate of the times, apart from the battle-cries which Mayakovski (to whose superhumanly inspiring presence the essays all testify) gave to art – the teaching and example of Meyerhold were crucial influences upon the development and formation of the Soviet cinema.

It was of course impossible for this aspect of Soviet cinema to be fully revealed in earlier publications. In 1940 Meyerhold was executed in Moscow during the Stalinist purges; his wife, the actress Zinaida Raikh, was murdered in their flat while he was still in prison. From this time until the middle of the 1950s every trace of Meyerhold's name was systematically erased from the history of the Soviet theatre, and with the Meyerhold archives hidden away and every reference, every recollection of his collaborators suppressed, the name was as effectively obliterated abroad as in his own country. His rehabilitation began about 1957 and proceeded gradually until quite recently the facts of his death were at last acknowledged and the charges made against him declared false. Today, with the Meyerhold archives once again available, it is possible to reassess his extraordinary achievement, his astonishing innovations in the theatre, his genius for rationalization, for fundamental analysis of the nature and problems of art – the gift of a great theorist for asking the right questions.

At first Meyerhold was not much taken by the cinema: in 1912 he wrote that 'there is no place for the cinematograph in the work of art, even in a purely auxiliary capacity'. Three years later he was evidently prepared to reconsider, for in 1915 he undertook to film *The Picture of Dorian Gray*. This and a succeeding film of Przybyszewski's novel *The Strong Man* are both lost, but the recollections of people who saw them at the time, and Meyerhold's own writings* suggest that they were as far ahead of contemporary film practice as his theatrical productions were in advance of the stage of his time. Meyerhold used the word 'art' in relation to the cinema, and that in itself was revolutionary. He perceived the need for inner rhythm, for a new form of acting, for the composition in light and texture of each shot. The development of a specifically cinematic form of acting fitted with the theories he was currently working out in his theatre, his insistence that the actor must achieve his effect through controlled techniques rather than the 'feeling' – the attempt actually to experience the emotions represented – advocated by the Stanislavsky school.

Oddly enough, after the Revolution, Meyerhold never directed another film, though there were innumerable projects – among them John Reed's *Ten Days That Shook the World*, which was to be filmed later by Meyerhold's pupil, Eisenstein. Yet the cinema continued to play an important role in Meyerhold's thinking. The magazine of his theatre (which Kozintsev here recalls reading as a boy) published regular articles on film – not just about Eisenstein and Vertov, but about Chaplin and Keaton, whose genius as a director was first recognized by Meyerhold.

As time went on his theatre work seems more and more to have been influenced by the cinema, in which he saw qualities, a power to stimulate the imagination, by and large absent from the theatre: 'something beyond the action which is vital to the theatre but indispensable to the cinema'. The 'something' of this remarkably modern notion was 'the ability of the film to play on the spectator's power of association'.

The quotation is from a lecture of 1936. Introducing Meyerhold on that occasion, Kozintsev said, 'The Soviet cinema learned much more than the Soviet theatre from the brilliant work of Meyerhold'; and he called Meyerhold 'our teacher', though he had never himself been his pupil. Others, though, had: among them the directors Eisenstein, Ekk, Yutkevitch, Roshal, Okhlopkov, Arnshtam; the actors Ilinski, Straukh, Martinson. All acknowledged their debt to him; and it must have taken some courage for Eisenstein to make reference to him in the essay included in this collection, written

---

* The reader is especially directed to Edward Braun's anthological study *Meyerhold on Theatre*, London and New York, 1969.

during the years of oblivion. While making obligatory acknowledgement of Meyerhold's political disgrace, he refers to him as 'my spiritual father . . . whose sandals I was unworthy to unlace (even allowing that he wore woolly boots in his unheated studio on the Novinski Boulevard)'.

Meyerhold's influence on his students and disciples shows most specifically in that cultivated 'eccentricism' which lends such vigour to their earliest films (Eisenstein's *Strike*, the work of the FEKS group); in the ability to relate a wide variety of artistic and theatrical experience – music-hall and Chinese theatre, circus and *commedia dell'arte*, folk art and jazz (it is revealed in the course of this book that the first jazz publicly performed in Russia was in fact in a Meyerhold production).

More broadly he taught them the method of isolating and exploring the fundamental and specific qualities of the cinema. He taught them a rationale and an aesthetic which re-emerges most brilliantly in the shorthand notes which have come down to us of Eisenstein's work as a teacher. Above all he instilled a sense of the *importance* of the cinema, its artistic equality – as the supreme heretic, he might have said superiority – to the theatre. This book is as much a tribute to Meyerhold as it is to the heroic age of the Soviet cinema.

Earlier I wrote that 'the brave youths of that time are old men now'. This is not exactly true. Some of course, like Golovnya, reveal in their writing only too clearly how much they have hardened into the prejudices of age; but the magic of the heroic days of revolutionary art is elsewhere persistent. Even in their sixties, Kozintsev and Yutkevitch and Romm still retain astonishing personal youthfulness: and the vitality of their writing comes from something more substantial than nostalgia – an enthusiasm and exaltation that survives intact from those days that were so astonishing and wonderful to them.

The texts in this volume are translations from the French *Le Cinéma Sovietique par ceux qui l'ont fait*, translated and edited by Luda and Jean Schnitzer and Marcel Martin; with reference to original Russian language versions where these exist. The section introductions have been augmented and revised; the introduction, glossary of persons and index are new to this English edition.

1. Sergei Iosipovitch Yutkevitch

Sergei Yutkevitch offers a remarkably vivid and evocative picture of the artistic world of Moscow in the early 1920s; of the economic privations of the period and, alongside, the unprecedented intellectual excitement generated among energetic youngsters, given a free hand, and enthusiastically seeking new forms of expression that could properly reflect the new social organizations. The search, as Yutkevitch reveals with characteristic humour, often resulted in somewhat wild aberrations and excesses; but no one, it seemed, could be dull in this atmosphere. The key influences for the young theatre artists of this generation were without question Mayakovski and Meyerhold: it was their example which led Eisenstein, Yutkevitch and their contemporaries to experiments in associating such disparate theatrical experiences as circus, puppets, fairground shows, music-hall and every genre of popular art – experiments which were later to prove of essential value in the development of Soviet cinema.

Like Kozintsev, Yutkevitch in his sixties still retains the vitality and the creative curiosity of the heroic years (compare his continuing willingness to experiment, in films like the animation version of Mayakovski's *The Bathhouse* and the highly stylized *Subject for a Short Story*). He is indeed one of the most attractive personalities in the Soviet cinema; and all his films bear the imprint of his personal charm and urbanity.

Born in 1904, as a boy Yutkevitch collaborated with Kozintsev and Alexei Kapler in presenting puppet shows in the streets of Kiev. He studied *mise en scène* with Mardjanov, and painting with Alexandra Exter. In 1922, in Leningrad (then Petrograd) he joined Kozintsev, Trauberg and Kryjitzki in the formation of FEKS (the Factory of the Eccentric Actor) and collaborated with them on the *Eccentric Manifesto*. The following year, in Moscow, he enrolled in Meyerhold's Studio at Vkhutemas.

He made his debut in the cinema in 1924, as director of an episode of *Give Us Radio!* In 1926 he was a writer and designer on Abram Room's *The Traitor*, and the following year, assistant and designer on Room's *Bed and Sofa*. His subsequent films have been *Lace* (1928), *The Black Veil* (1929), *The Golden Mountains* (1931; his first sound film, with a score by Shostakovitch), *Counterplan* (1932, co-directed with Ermler and Arnshtam), *Ankara, Heart of Turkey* (1934), *Miners* (1937), *How the Elector Will Vote* (1937), *The Man With the Gun* (1938), *Yakov Sverdlov* (1940), *Film Notes on Battle No 7* (1941), *The New Adventures of the Good Soldier Schweik* (1942), *Liberated France* (1944), *Hello, Moscow!* (1945), *Our Country's Youth* (1946), an episode of *Three Meetings* (1948), *Prjevalsky* (1951), *Skanderbeg* (1953), *Othello* (1958), *Yves Montand Sings* (1957, co-director with M. Slutzky), *Stories About Lenin* (1957), *Meeting With France* (1960), *The Bathhouse* (1962), *Peace to your House* (animation film, 1963), *Lenin in Poland* (1966), *Subject for a Short Story* (1969).

Yutkevitch's revivals of Mayakovski's *The Bathhouse* (1954) and *The Bed Bug* (1956) at the Moscow Satire Theatre were a revelation in the Soviet theatre of those times, resuming, as they did, a line of activity that had been cut short with the death of Meyerhold in 1940.

Teenage Artists of the Revolution

They were astonishing and wonderful days – the beginnings of a revolutionary art. When we talk about the years when we started artistic work, people are always surprised by the birth-dates of almost all the directors and the major artists of those times. We were incredibly young! We were sixteen- and seventeen-year-olds when we entered upon our artistic lives. The explanation is quite simple: the Revolution had made way for the young. It has to be remembered that an entire generation had disappeared. Our elders had been dispersed throughout the country, or had perished in the Civil War, or had left Russia. Hence the Republic lacked a clear organization, lacked people; and our way in was easy – the country wanted us to work, the country needed people in every department of culture.

This was a period of tumultuous expansion for Soviet art. It is difficult now to imagine how it was . . . in Leningrad, for instance, in 1919 or 1920, the former capital of the Russian empire, deserted but still beautiful. Victor Shklovski describes the period, how the grass grew on the sidewalks and between the stones of the road . . . which is all true: but at the same time the city was experiencing an intense cultural life. There had never been so many theatres (and incidentally, at that time theatres were free); never had so many books – particularly volumes of poetry – appeared. Never had there been so much experiment in the theatre and in painting. I remember for instance a

Sergei Yutkevitch

theatre where we went as young boys that was quite astonishing, though unhappily only short-lived, called the Theatre of Popular Comedy. It had been established by the producer Sergei Radlov, a great expert of classical theatre and an extremely cultured and bookish man who had been obliged to fall in step with the epoch.

In the immense 'iron room', as it was called, of the House of the People which had been created before the Revolution, Radlov had organized his theatre, for which he had hired circus performers as actors. There were also a few professional players, among them the wife of Alexander Blok, Lyuba Bassargina-Blok. But most of the actors came from the circus. Radlov discovered truly remarkable acting talents in these circus performers.

The theatre's repertory was extremely original. For a start, Radlov was one of the first to present some of the old pantomimes of Deburau. Curiously enough it was a clown, Alexander Sergeyevich Alexandrov, who appeared under the stage name of Serge, who proved the most extraordinary interpreter of the role of Pierrot. At this theatre I saw for the first time a traditional Pierrot; for Radlov's pantomimes were re-created from authentic transcripts of the presentations of the old Théâtre des Funambules.

Apart from these, Radlov's theatre presented Molière, Shakespeare and so on – but still played by circus performers. Most interesting though were the plays which Radlov himself wrote. I remember one called *Love and Gold*. These plays were fantasies which combined adventure stories with strongly defined social themes. The action might be set in Russia, in Paris or in an imaginary New York, with improbable chases, scuffles, transformation scenes and such like. . . . . In short they were fascinating experiments in assembling all sorts of elements from the modern theatre, perhaps influenced by French adventure serials like *Les Vampires* or *Fantomas* or the American equivalents which had just begun to appear on our screens: *The Iron Claw* (1916), *The Fatal Ring* (1917), and other Pearl White films. Elements from traditional French pantomime, from the theatre of the fairgrounds, the Shakespearean stage, and the Tabarin farces were all mixed together to give birth to a truly popular theatre. The audience at that time was largely composed of what were ironically known as 'cigarette merchants'. These were youngsters who sold cigarettes singly or as tab-ends – the 'gamins' of revolutionary Leningrad.

Naturally the theatre was equally patronized by the intellectuals, writers, artists . . . but there were also the workers and soldiers. It really was a popular audience. And Radlov, refined aesthete though he was, offered this public an extraordinarily interesting experience – the first experience of a popular theatre.

At that time, too, Leningrad produced an entirely unique kind of spectacle – the mass street performances. *The Taking of the Winter Palace* was a haunting reconstruction of real-life events in the actual historical locations; a sort of mystery play performed in the Palace square and on the steps of the Bourse, with the participation of real warships, marine detachments, and with classical choirs (one might well ask why) and masks representing capitalists and proletarians.

I recall another spectacle, on the Isles – on all three at once – off the coast of the Baltic Gulf. At the end of Red Dawn Street – as the former Kamennoostrovsky Prospect had been renamed – a vast amphitheatre had been created, and beyond, on these three islands, a fantastic spectacle was presented, rather like the classical spectacles, with the participation of boats, warships, military detachments, the whole concluding with an immense firework display.

I feel that this attempt to create mass spectacles was a continuation of the tradition begun by Mayakovski with his *Mystère-Bouffe*. It was subsequently to have a great influence on the films of Eisenstein. For there is no doubt that *Strike* and *The Battleship Potemkin* are in direct line of descent from this genre of popular spectacle, born out of the Revolution.

What were the most significant and interesting features of the art of this epoch? First of all, as I have said, total freedom for experiment. Nothing was yet stabilized. The Republic had scarcely finished with the Civil War; it was only beginning to create its own culture; and the doors were wide open for anyone who wanted to work with the Soviet power. Not that everything was easy in those times. There were some among the older generation who, whilst accepting posts in the theatre or elsewhere from the State, were in practice sabotaging the ideas of Soviet power. The young ones were meanwhile, of course, going forward open-heartedly.

At this time a memorable journal was created: it was called *Art of the Commune*, and had as its founders Mayakovski, Brik and Punin, who called themselves 'the komfuts' – the communist-futurists. Here were published Mayakovski's first 'Orders to the Army of Art'. Incidentally, at this period newspapers were not sold, but were stuck up on walls so that everyone could read them. Bread and tramways were also free – just as were the theatres.

So it was in this atmosphere of research, trial and experiment that the new art of the Soviet State was born. It was an extremely motley art, subject to every influence, to every breath of the winds which had only just begun to filter through from the West. We had only just begun to learn what was going on in the rest of Europe.

But what is curious is that comparable experiments – particularly in the theatre – appeared simultaneously in Moscow and Paris, but without any direct link . . . for instance all that Radlov was doing, all that Annenkov was doing with the 'kinetic décors' which he created for the expressionist plays of Toller and Kaiser. (Since there was no national modern dramaturgy, the expressionist dramaturgy was at that time admitted as being revolutionary.) 'Kinetic décors' were so called by their creator because they moved on stage. Radlov's costumes, Annenkov's costumes, our costumes at the Foregger Theatre, Meyerhold's costumes resembled to a surprising degree the costumes designed by Picasso for *Parade* or those which Cocteau had created for Diaghilev. Altogether there was a strange coincidence between what we were doing and the experiments that were being carried out in Paris, and which we only knew about much later.

The reason is that in its search for new directions, the whole young generation of Soviet artists had turned towards minor genres, the kind of popular art which the aristocracy and bourgeoisie had scorned. To be precise: the music-hall, the circus and the cinema. To all these genres, hitherto considered 'in poor taste', the Revolution had opened up entirely new possibilities; and they became particularly influential.

From all this was born the movement which we christened 'Eccentricism'. It was, it must now be confessed, a strange mixture of mere aberrations and of juvenile passion for the circus burlesque, which for us carried echoes of the tradition of Deburau. We had just seen the first films of Chaplin and this was at once a revelation and an extension of the line of the music-hall and circus. At the same time the first German expressionist pictures had just appeared on our screens. They had a great influence on us all. I recall how with Eisenstein I saw Lang's *Doctor Mabuse* for the first time, and what a profound effect it had on both of us. It is worth recalling that Eisenstein learned editing from this film: Esther Shub, who taught both of us editing, had to re-edit the film and Eisenstein appointed himself her voluntary assistant in order to be able to study the construction of Fritz Lang's montage.

It was also with Eisenstein that I first saw *Intolerance*, in 1921, I believe. At that time the public did not understand the whole complexity of Griffith's film, the way in which it manipulated space and time. Part of the audience demonstrated noisily, believing that the projectionist had mixed up the reels. But we two were absolutely bowled over by what was for us a revelation.

We were also great enthusiasts for the French and American serials. In this connection it is interesting to note that Eisenstein attached an immense importance to the study of the mechanics of 'distractive' art, to the analysis of the means which the masters of the genre employed to act upon their audiences. The aim was not to imitate them, but to oppose our own, new art to theirs, taking advantage of the study of works of the past.

The myths propagated by our opponents, who claimed that Soviet art denied and demolished all that had gone before, are only the invention of the ignorant. Certainly we wanted to build anew, but I think we knew quite well the art of the past, art which taught us a great deal. Although co-opted by the 'Proletcult', an organization whose whole concept denied the art of the past (a position in fact forcefully criticized by Lenin) Eisenstein in particular believed that the new theatre must be born precisely from deep study of all the culture of the past, from a complete knowledge of the theatre, literature and cinema.

He had asked me to give a series of lectures on a specific subject: 'The adventure film and detective literature.' I was to explain to the young fellows who had come to 'Proletcult' straight from the country or even from the front, the cultural heritage that they had to assimilate – and overcome. I worked out a course on the construction of the detective novel, beginning with the classics, especially the French: Ponson de Terrail, Gaboriau, Leblanc, Gaston Leroux, etc., explaining what were the sources of the 'distractions', how they went about attracting attention, how to construct a compelling intrigue and dénouement – all the secrets of the author's methods. In the same way I analysed the structure of adventure films, especially serials. All this was later to be of the greatest service to my audiences' generation! Among them were Grigori Alexandrov, Maxim Straukh, Judith Gliese and many others who have since become illustrious artists, recognized by the Republic. These bright-eyed girls and boys hungrily absorbed the whole enormous diversity of bourgeois culture. Eisenstein, of course, was a man of immense culture, who spoke four languages perfectly. He less than anyone maintained a nihilist position towards culture. What is characteristic is this intrusion of new elements into the old, aesthetic elements coming from the so-called minor genres of the circus, music-hall and films. This was notable in all the stage productions and all the films of these first years.

Eisenstein made his début with a production of *The Mexican*, inspired by the Jack London novel. Officially the director was Smichliayev and Eisenstein was only the designer; but in fact this was his first work of direction. He did not by accident devise the boxing match which was presented in front of the drop curtain. The original plan was to have the boxing match take place off-stage, in the traditional manner, only the reactions of the characters being shown. Eisenstein wished to counter bourgeois 'distractive' art with a pure sporting spectacle. He built a proper ring in the proscenium, taught the actors to box properly – a tremendously exciting spectacle – and he appeared extremely proud of having been the first to introduce an authentic sports exhibition in a legitimate theatrical presentation. It was the same kind of daring as when Picasso or Braque introduced bits of coloured paper or fragments of newspaper into their pictures, when 'collage' made its appearance and people dared to introduce new elements, never hitherto utilized, into painting.

So our infatuation for the circus, music-hall and cinema was not a chance thing, but led us to overturn all aesthetic concepts and create a new aesthetic of the revolutionary spectacle. From this resulted on the one hand the mass spectacles and popular shows, and on the other the introduction of minor genres into classical art forms. Quite definitely the reactionaries at that time were those whom we now call abstract artists. We called them 'suprematists', which was the term introduced by Malevitch. Later the painter Tatlin called his first works 'counter-reliefs'. . . . Basically the analytical current in figurative art had reached an extreme point.

In 1922 Kozintsev and I exhibited in the 'Left Stream Exhibition' in Leningrad, which included not only the famous 'Black and White Square', but also another picture by Tatlin which represented nothing at all – the canvas was simply and uniformly covered with a wash of pink paint. That was really the end of the line.

Our paintings, mine and Kozintsev's, were hung side by side: joyous collages, posters representing circus people and eccentric actors, made up of fragments of other posters. Variegated mosaics, strong in colour – works which, when you come down to it, were also impertinent and eccentric.

And they earned us criticism, because already a certain academism was making itself felt among the movements of the Left. I recall Punin, the theorist of the movement, saying to us scornfully, 'If you go on in this fashion you'll end up in the cinema.' The cinema was the lowest rank in the hierarchy of the arts. Or rather, which was worse, it did not even have a place therein!

In such circumstances, then, were born simultaneously the experiments of Annenkov in Leningrad, the productions of Meyerhold in Moscow and the beginnings of the theatre of Foregger, a novel mixture of political revue and the songs of Mistinguette. The music of 'Mon homme', a tremendous novelty, reached us rather oddly by way of *Lef* – Lili Brik having brought it from Paris. It was, I repeat, a fantastic medley of revolutionary themes, American-style vaudeville, adventure films, abstract art and . . . the highest art of theatrical design.

Constructivism had just been born and had an enormous influence on theatrical production, with moving and changing décors. Everyone rushed to the Kamerny Theatre to see the set which the architect Vesnin had devised for the stage adaptation of Chesterton's *The Man Who Was Thursday* and which had real lifts going up and down. In Meyerhold's production of

Kozintsev: costume for a stage production, 1920

Crommelynck's *The Magnanimous Cuckold* great wheels turned. For Soukhovo-Kobyline's *The Death of Tarelkin*, in the constructivist Varvara Stepanova had created a set entirely mounted on springs. When people sat on tables or chairs they would first of all recoil under the actor's weight to the level of the stage, then spring back and eject the person sitting on them. Better still: the furnishings were all fitted with crackers, so that they produced a frightful din on the stage.

It was such bold experiments in the most varied departments of stage and cinema art which led to the organization of Kuleshov's Studio, to our own FEKS Theatre and also to the creation of a very curious theatre which practically no one remembers now: The 'Heroic Experimental Theatre'

19

directed by Boris Ferdinandov, a former Tairov actor. He propounded the theory that the theatre can *only* be heroic. His repertoire began with *Oedipus Rex*. Moreover he insisted that speech and gesture must be rigorously rhythmic. Consequently his actors behaved on the stage like so many marionettes, playing according to an exact scheme of movements laid down by the director. The result was quite surprising. It must be added that Sophocles was played in constructivist décors, with masks; and that the words also were subordinated to the inexorable rules of the 'master-rhythm'. Subsequently Ferdinandov presented still more astonishing spectacles, such as Labiche's *La Cagnotte*, acted in the same manner with strictly rhythmical speech; and a modern melodrama, *The Lady with the Black Glove*, written by the imagist poet Vadim Cherchenevitch, a continuation of Radlov's experiments in the creation of a melodrama that should be at once modern and fantastic.

I have only been able to mention a few aspects; but this was the atmosphere in which was born this new art – art which often went astray, and had in it many elements which it was subsequently to discard. It seems to me though that within it such art carried the force of our conviction: a new revolutionary content demanded new forms, equally revolutionary. And these researches in the most varied areas were later to permit those of us who were concerned to create the art of socialist realism to use them while giving them a new quality.

And so something which happened later was not accidental: in the spring of 1941 Eisenstein and I both received our first awards from the State – from the hands of Nemirovitch-Danchenko, and in that same Moscow Art Theatre against which we had once fought so vigorously, opposing our new revolutionary theatre to the theatre and to naturalistic art. Eisenstein and I, for fun, totted up the prize-winners, and discovered that eighty per cent were artists of our own generation, all pupils of Meyerhold. All had taken part in the fantastic experiments of revolutionary art! These experiments may seem naive, bizarre, ridiculous, insolent, even totally incomprehensible today. But all the same they played their part in the era in which was born that art which is the glory of our country.

(Interview recorded in Paris, 29 May 1966)

The Sorcerer's Apprentices

I first met Sergei Mikhailovitch Eisenstein in August 1921. This was in the course of the entrance examinations for *mise en scène* for the State Studios, which were known, abbreviations being then the style, as GVYRM. GVYRM had been Meyerhold's idea. He had just concluded the 1920–1 season at the First RSFSR Theatre – a season which had proved stormy as a result of two extremely controversial productions: *Dawn* and Mayakovski's *Mystère-Bouffe*.

Meyerhold's slogan of 'Theatrical October' produced a marked schism in the artistic intelligentsia and resulted in the clear definition of two distinct

Sergei Eisenstein (*c.* 1921)

currents in the theatre. The right wing grouped together the academic theatres (including the Kamerny and Tairov theatres); the supporters of the left wing were Meyerhold's own theatre, the Proletcult Theatre – which ironically was situated in the 'Ermitage', the very place where the Moscow Art Theatre had originated – Foregger's Studio and the Studio of Ferdinandov's Heroic-Experimental Theatre.

All these theatres were just gathering their forces together in 1921; in the following year they were to combine to organize the Left Front. The First RSFSR Theatre had no solid commercial foundation and no permanent company. When it was merged with the former Nezlobin Dramatic Theatre, and this new organization had to face the problem of mounting new productions – and all this was happening at the beginning of NEP – Meyerhold withdrew from work in the theatre, leaving it in charge of his closest collaborator, V. M. Bebutov. Meyerhold himself had decided to form an army of young people before launching a fresh attack upon the academic theatres.

This was an old and tried method for Meyerhold. He liked experimental studio work in the course of which he could discover and then verify the principles which he would subsequently transfer to the theatre.

Thus it was that in the autumn of 1921 we found ourselves in the tiny hall of a mansion in the Novinski Boulevard, which had previously been a school. Meyerhold and his family were living there in a small apartment on the second or third floor. Thence a minute and creaking wooden lift led to a classroom in which were lines of plain school desks. This classroom and the small hall were the entire premises of GVYRM.

In the hall, behind the table of the admissions board, Meyerhold himself presided. He was wearing a faded pullover, soldiers' puttees over his trousers and enormous thick-soled shoes. He had a woollen scarf around his neck and from time to time would put a red fez on his head.

By his side was a man who was totally bald, with a very neat red beard, piercing eyes and rapid movements: Ivan Alexandrovitch Aksenov, a poet of the oddly named 'Centrifugal' group and the author of the first monograph in Russian on Picasso, with the unusual title of *Picasso and his Environs*. He was also a translator (Meyerhold's production of *The Magnanimous Cuckold* was done from his version) and a brilliant and erudite scholar, particularly in respect of the Elizabethan theatre.

Next to him was another entirely bald man, ascetic and monk-like in appearance: Valeri Bebutov. At the side was a Mongol, small but stocky. This was Valeri Inkidjinov, who was to become famous for his playing in Pudovkin's *Storm Over Asia*. Regarded as the great specialist in movement, Inkidjinov was Meyerhold's principal collaborator in this department.

We had to present ourselves before this tribunal. In the Cyrillic alphabet my name and Eisenstein's begin with adjacent letters. At the same time as myself, then, there arrived a rather stumpy young man, with his hair on end rather like a clown, with an enormous forehead and bright, ironic eyes. Not having heard his name properly I called him Eisenstadt.

With one movement we presented our portfolios of drawings to the Areopagus. They asked us a few questions, then we were free until the next day, when the examinations proper were to take place.

Left alone, Eisenstein and I began by getting the pronunciation of our respective names clear. Then we discovered that we were linked by the common professions of painter and scene designer.

I immediately recalled the name of Eisenstein which I had read on the handbills of the Proletcult Workers' Theatre, where it appeared together with that of the painter Nikitin as one of the designers of the quite recent production of *The Mexican*, after Jack London.

We sat on a bench on the Novinski Boulevard, in the shade of the leafy trees which then lined it. I soon learned the uncomplicated biography of my new friend. He was six years older than myself, a native of Riga, had studied at the Architectural Institute, joined the Red Army, been demobilized and, arriving in Moscow, had simultaneously set himself to learn Japanese and to work as a designer in the Proletcult Theatre. Like myself he dreamed of becoming *metteur en scène* and it was this which had brought him to Meyerhold.

The following day the examinations, which were very simple but rather unusual, began. After a cross-examination designed to assess our cultural level, Eisenstein and myself were given the same problem to solve: on a blackboard we had to design the following *mise en scène*: six characters in pursuit of one.

I can remember Eisenstein's solution. He drew with the chalk a kind of pavilion with six doors (I recalled the scene a few years later when I saw the wine-jar scene in Meyerhold's production of *The Government Inspector*). Then, with rapid lines, he planned the scene of an elaborate *mise en scène* which recalled the trick transformations of the Italian clown Fregoli.

Since the Meyerhold theatre demands that a *metteur en scène* must also possess the technique of an actor, we were also tested for our 'expressiveness'. Both had to shoot an arrow from an imaginary bow.

The following day we were informed that we had both been accepted into GVYRM.

From the first lesson, Eisenstein and I had grabbed the front desk, practically touching the Master's table. Meyerhold appeared. He scrutinized us with his piercing gaze, and announced that we were going to study two subjects: *mise en scène* and Biomechanics. This was the first time that we had heard this bizarre word which designated a new system of expressive stage movement. Meyerhold told us that Biomechanics were still in an experimental stage and that he was going to work out the fundamentals with us.

Meyerhold's teaching of *mise en scène* took an equally original form. He wished to establish a purely scientific theory: 'The theory of the creation of a spectacle.' He affirmed that the *metteur en scène*'s whole process of creation must resolve into formulas, and he encouraged us to trace *schemas*, to elaborate a kind of scientific systematization of all the stages from the birth of a production.

He became very enthusiastic and improvised appropriately, painting the picture of a sort of ideal *metteur en scène* who, in his view, must himself direct the production like an orchestra conductor. He presented to us the image of a theatre in which the *metteur en scène* occupies a desk equipped with an innumerable array of levers and buttons.

The *metteur en scène*, according to Meyerhold, must 'listen attentively to the reactions of the audience, and by means of an extremely complex system of signals, modify the rhythms of the performance according to the reactions of the spectators'. He dreamed of the possibility of speeding-up or slowing-down the rhythm of the actor's playing: 'If today's audience accepts this pause, then prolong it. You will only have to press such and such a button!'

It was fascinating to watch this born improviser trying to inculcate in us a system which, according to his propositions, would leave no place for anything unplanned.

After a few lessons, Eisenstein confided to me that he had had enough of drawing circles and squares and that he intended to wake Meyerhold up a bit and force him to unveil the true *cuisine* of his creation.

When the bell announced the end of the lesson, we asked Meyerhold if he would stay behind a bit to answer some additional questions. That year Meyerhold was not working in the theatre, and devoted all his time to us. He was in no hurry to leave and willingly stayed behind. We asked him to talk about specific productions. We wanted to know how the plan for the *mise en scène* of Blok's *Balaganchik* at the Kommissarjevskaia Theatre had come about, and how he had worked with Ida Rubinstein on the production of d'Annunzio's *Pisanella* in Paris, and many other things relating to his immensely rich experience as a *metteur en scène*.

Our curiosity excited Meyerhold. He warmed to it and started to tell us earnestly and in great detail a host of astonishing things. Thus it was that bit by bit we managed to divert our teacher from his taste for *schemas*. His classes were fed by an irresistible fantasy. He would describe not only the productions which he had realized, but also those which he wanted to mount. Thus we heard him talk for the first time about a project for *Hamlet* which unhappily was never realized by Meyerhold himself. These lessons did us enormous good, and Eisenstein always said that it was through these talks of Meyerhold's that he first understood what *mise en scène* really is.

One day Meyerhold came into the classroom with a young woman with short hair, a leather jacket and men's boots. He said: 'I want to introduce Zinaida Essenina-Raikh, my assistant in Biomechanics. Today is the first lesson.' He had us go into the hall and line up face to face in pairs. Eisenstein and I found ourselves together.

Meyerhold himself demonstrated the first exercise, which is very difficult to describe since its point lay in the maximum of expressiveness and the 'rationale' of each movement. It was the sort of acrobatic play one associates with circus clowns. One of the partners taunted the other. The second would make a spring, cross the room at a run and aim an imaginary blow at the nose of his adversary with his foot. The adversary would reply with an imaginary blow; and he would fall down. Then the partners changed places.

Meyerhold himself did this exercise with quite impeccable neatness and expressiveness. The exercise effectively brought into play a whole series of movements which tended to a certain logistic. It introduced such elements as 'refusal of obstacle', balance, rational movements, rhythm and so on.

Meyerhold was a fierce opponent of what he called 'Duncanism', that is to say of all demonstrative plasticity, of the 'danced' emotional affectation, in short of all that delighted the *habitués* of various studios of ballet and rhythmic dance. In the same way he was against Delsarte. There was no stylization in Biomechanics, which was based on pantomime borrowed from the *commedia dell'arte* and the acrobatic circus.

The exercises which Inkidjinov and Zinaida Raikh made us do when Meyerhold was not present became daily more complicated. They demanded a more and more intense physical training, to which regular lessons in acrobatics contributed.

There, too, Eisenstein and myself linked up, and, with application, forced ourselves to overcome the natural inertia of our bodies. That was until one day when Eisenstein, who was supposed to be my 'catcher', let his mind wander, so that I practically broke my neck falling after a dangerous jump.

After that we carefully avoided acrobatics, claiming that we had adequately assimilated the basics.

Then the season opened at the First RSFSR Theatre. Bebutov had produced Ibsen's *The League of Youth*, in which our entire class performed each evening an extremely complicated quadrille. We had no need even to make up. The director's idea was that the ball should be masked, and so having put on our masks I whirled with Eisenstein in the farandole.

But while we were serving our apprenticeship with Meyerhold we still had to think about our daily bread. There were no scholarships at this time. They were difficult years. . . . Our student rations were somewhat meagre. We mostly ate potato fritters which my good mother cooked on the stove which we then called 'bourgeoise'. This is why Eisenstein and myself concluded an agreement that the first of us who found work would engage the other as a collaborator.

I was the first to have some luck. A theatre critic, Samouil Margolin, a fiery enthusiast with masses of hair and eyes like live coals, and who wrote enthusiastic articles about the 'Leftist' theatre, decided to become a director and entered the Third Moscow Art Theatre Studio under Yevgeni Vakhtangov. To gain admission he had to present a project for a production, accompanied by designs. He could not draw and asked me, as a favour, to do some designs for him for two Molière plays, *La Jalousie de Barbouille* and *Le Médecin Volant*. I did the designs, which Margolin pinned on the walls of his room. The *metteur en scène* Foregger and the dramatist Mass, visiting him, saw the drawings. They liked them and asked me to do the décors for their new production. I accepted on condition that I could work together with Eisenstein. Foregger made no objection. So we became the designers for a new theatre which was called the Foregger Studio – Masterskaia Foreggera, or in abbreviation, Mastfor.

Foregger was a very strange person. Coming from a Russified German family, his full name was Baron Foregger von Greiffenturn. He was a lean and elegant young man, always dressed in the latest fashion, and extremely short-sighted so that he had to wear big glasses with horn rims. He spoke Russian well, but could not master the characteristic Russian hard 'l', which gave him a foreign intonation. After graduating from the philology faculty of Kiev University, Foregger became interested in the theatre, and a true connoisseur of the classical drama. His first productions were actually revivals of the *commedia dell'arte* and of medieval French farces, particularly Tabarin.

Arriving in Moscow at the start of the Revolution, he began by opening a theatre in his own home. At this period there was an incredible number of little theatres and studios, and no one was really surprised that his Theatre of the Four Masks should operate in a private flat. In just the same way the 'Semperante' Theatre, then very well known, functioned in the two-roomed flat belonging to Levchina and Bykov, who were directors and actors in this temple of improvisation.

The Theatre of the Four Masks closed after a few performances; but as a result of its activity, Foregger encountered the dramatist Vladimir Mass. Together they decided that pure revivalism of the old classical theatre could no longer be of any value, and that it was necessary to create a new comedy of masks.

Observing the tradition that a theatre mask must be the generalized expression of real-life people, Foregger and Mass invented the following types: 'The Merchant' (typical of the NEP period); 'The girl communist with the leather brief-case' (satirizing the leather-jacketed woman who spoke only in slogans and militated, in imitation of Kollontai, for 'the theory of free love'); 'The Intellectual Mystic' (of which the prototype was partly the poet Andréi Bélyi, partly other eccentric Muscovites – they still exist); 'The Imagist Poet' (a kind of quintessence both of the peasant poet of the Essenin variety and of the 'dandy' of the Mariengov or Cherchenevitch type); 'The Militiaman', guardian of law and order; and finally, the simple clown, 'The Auguste' who gets under the feet of everyone else.

These masks or types, plus other characters introduced according to the needs of topicality, formed the skeleton for the first show, entitled *How They Mustered*, which had for its subject the foreign intervention against the young Soviet State.

It was in the studio at Vkhutemas (the abbreviated form of the name of the Higher Institute of Arts and Techniques), with the actors playing on a stage improvised from tables put end to end, that I saw for the first time, in the audience, Mayakovski. I don't recall how he was dressed. All that has stayed in my memory is a big, thick walking-stick with a curved handle, which I was often to see later, meeting him in the streets of Moscow.

The performance evidently pleased Mayakovski. He applauded with his enormous hands, and after the performance I heard him rumbling something encouraging, in his bass voice, to the students who clustered round him, and to the lean, bespectacled Foregger. Eisenstein and I had to do the sets for a *Parody Show* about currently fashionable theatrical productions. It was in three parts: 'For Every Wise Man One Operetta is Enough', which rather wickedly derided the infatuation of Nemirovitch-Danchenko of the Moscow Art Theatre with *La Fille de Madame Angot*; 'Don't Drink Water Unless it's Been Boiled', a parody of the then popular propaganda plays; and a parody of the production of Claudel's *L'Annonce faite à Marie* which Tairov had just done at the Kamerny Theatre. As it happened only this last play required décors. Naturally our young theatre had no money, while we needed décors at once funny and pompous, parodying the style of the painter Vesnin.

On reflection Eisenstein and myself decided to try a new method. We got hold of a quantity of brightly coloured paper which we stuck on to cardboard forms, parodying the cubist settings of Vesnin. This provided a portable and extremely lively décor. Our work was considerably admired, and Foregger entrusted us with the designs for his new play. This, written by Mass, was called *Be Kind to the Horses*. The title was taken from the famous poem by

Mayakovski, and of course had nothing at all to do with horses. The play was in two parts: in the first the masks or types already mentioned went through some business which was fairly thin, but stuffed with topical jokes and references. The second part was a parody of a music-hall performance. I did the sets; Eisenstein the costumes. As always he displayed a prodigal imagination, particularly in the costumes for the music-hall numbers.

For the actresses who did a singing turn, in place of skirts he devised large hoops of wire, suspended on multi-coloured ribbons. The ribbons were placed at considerable intervals, so that the astonished Muscovite spectators, who had been rather ascetically brought up in these years, could descry beneath them the slim lines of the actresses' legs. About six months later, the painter Jakulov used the same idea for the costumes of the operetta *Girofle-Girofla* at the Kamerny. Eisenstein, I remember, was extremely annoyed at the plagiarism, and even wanted to write a letter of protest to the editors of the *Theatrical Journal*.

He showed similar wit in his costume for 'The Imagist Poet'. Eisenstein divided him in two parts: the left half was dressed in a peasant shirt, full trousers and a boot; the right half wore a stylish frock-coat.

The première took place on New Year's Eve 1922, in the House of the Press (now the House of Journalists) on Nikitsky Boulevard. It was a great success, and Eisenstein and I had a good press.

A few weeks later, at the same place, there was a debate devoted to *Be Kind to the Horses*. At that time, of course, there were practically daily debates, on every possible subject, with discussion which worked up to a white heat of passion. This was the case with our production. Viatcheslav Polonski, then editor of the magazine *The Press and the Revolution*, attacked *Be Kind to the Horses*.

Then Mayakovski went on to the little stage of the House of the Press, and proceeded to demolish Polonski with his defence of the show. It was there that I first heard my own name spoken in public. The poet congratulated Eisenstein on his costumes, and me for the sets which in every possible respect might be calculated to offend Polonski, since they represented an 'urbanist' landscape in the brutal manner of posters and, moreover, were 'kinetic' in the sense that isolated sections of the backcloth moved by means of the most primitive kind of 'mechanization' – manually operated, naturally!

Mayakovski was concerned with everything. We saw him very often, practically every day, either at the House of the Press, or at Meyerhold's rehearsals, or at Vkhutemas. He might have been a patrol leader doing an inspection of his sentries, making sure that everyone who was defending the ideals of revolutionary art was really at his post.

In the autumn of 1922 our little theatre definitively took the name of 'Mastfor', and was installed in its own premises, at No. 7 Arbat. At this time the lobby of the theatre was called the 'vauxhall'. After the premières, we arranged parties which were attended by everyone who was anyone in the theatrical and artistic world of Moscow. Mayakovski and Lili and Osip Brik came to all the premières and naturally were guests at these parties. But Mayakovski would appear in the lobby during the daytime, too. He was fascinated to see the actors practising under the direction of the dancer Ferry (one would then hardly have predicted that we were soon to know him under the name of Fedor Bogordski, a painter who was to achieve resounding success with his paintings of the 'bezprizornyi' – the abandoned children of the revolutionary era); or to see them taking lessons from the well-known boxing champion Boris Barnet (at that time he had not even begun to work as an actor with Kuleshov, still less thought of becoming a film director).

At this time we were joined by Vladimir Fogel, who was to become a very remarkable cinema actor, and Alexander Matcheret, who combined his work as a débutant actor with his function as a legal counsellor to the Moscow Executive Committee. Also attached to our theatre were the actress and dancer Ludmilla Semyonova and Ivan Chuveliov (both of whom were to become well known in the cinema), Boris Poslavski, another remarkable film actor, Natalia Lvova, later an actress of the Vakhtangov Theatre, Vitali Jemchujnyi (who made several features and now makes scientific films) and many more – gifted and lively contemporaries of my youth.

Mayakovski was a friend to all the active young, and followed everyone's progress; and to feel that he was the friend of our theatre helped make our work better and more enjoyable.

Meyerhold began to eye us a little wryly. He could not forbid us to work as designers, but he became jealous of Foregger. Shortly before the première of *Be Kind to the Horses* something happened which was of enormous importance to Eisenstein and myself. Meyerhold announced that for one evening the course was suspended and that we were going in a group to see the production of *The Mexican* at the Proletcult Theatre. Eisenstein was very moved. For the first time the Master consented to look at the work of one of his pupils.

I recall how we were installed in a cluster in the front row of the circle of the Ermitage Theatre. Eisenstein sat beside me; and his hands were frozen with nerves.

The show turned out to be extremely interesting. It was at once apparent where the director Smichliayev and his passably eclectic inventions ended and where Eisenstein began.

The first scene, which was set in Mexico, was feebly conceived, and does not remain in my memory. The key to the production was the second part. Eisenstein had arranged on the stage the two offices of two rival boxing promoters. Wanting to emphasize in a satirical way the dehumanized, mechanized aspect of transatlantic civilization, he had decided, with his usual sense of invention and his maximalism, to give one of the offices only square forms, and the other only round ones. This applied not only to the furnishings, but also to the characters, transformed either into spheres or cubes by their costumes and even their make-up. Kelly, the boss of one of the offices, had a round costume, a round wig, circular forms stuck on his cheeks

Trauberg, Yutkevitch and Kozintsev (l. to r.) in 1922

and make-up. The other, whose name I forget, was entirely made into cubic form. In contrast to these stylized figures, the hero of the play, the Mexican Rivera, entered through the auditorium, without any make-up; and when he removed his black cloak and broad-brimmed hat, appeared before us as a slim, brown-haired adolescent, the only living man in this collection of dolls.

Meyerhold liked the production; and so did the rest of us. Eisenstein glowed.

Not long after this I left for Leningrad, where, with Grigori Kozintsev and Leonid Trauberg, I took part in organizing FEKS, or the Factory of the Eccentric Actor. Eisenstein stayed in Moscow and designed the costumes for Foregger's next production, *The Child Snatcher*, a melodrama by Ennery. This ancient melodrama was directed by Foregger in an excessively rapid rhythm, as a 'cinematographic' spectacle. He lit it with projectors in front of which he had rapidly turning shutters, so as to give the impression of the flickering light of a silent projector.

At this time Eisenstein and myself exchanged interminable letters, describing all the artistic novelties of the two capitals and which we signed with the weird pseudonym 'Pipifax'. It was a joke name in the fashion of clowns – we were crazy about the circus. Eisenstein was 'Pipi' and I was 'Fax'.

Soon I had an urgent call from my friend, asking me to come to Moscow. Our original bargain still applied, and this time it was Eisenstein who had got the commission. The producer V. Tikhonovitch wanted to do *Macbeth* at the Central Educational Theatre. The part of Lady Macbeth was to be played by his wife, a provincial actress. The place selected, by necessity, was very unsuitable for a theatre. But the job of doing sets for the Shakespearean tragedy was too tempting, and we went to work enthusiastically.

The director had no clear idea on how he was to mount *Macbeth*. We suggested the following solution: there should be no drop-curtain, and the play should be presented in a single architectural setting which could be transformed to an extent by props brought onto the stage. We built a platform. In the centre we placed an enormous, tower-like torch. According to the needs of the action, this torch served as the sentinel's lodge, or the castle entry, for it was surrounded by a spiral stairway. We also proposed to eliminate all colour from the setting, which was entirely hung with neutral grey canvas. Only the lighting and the colour of the sky on the backcloth was to change. The entire tonal range of the production was to be restricted to three colours: black, gold and purple.

An attentive student of Eisenstein's art can perceive from studying his sketches for *Macbeth* the continuity and perseverance with which he worked at the images which excited his creative imagination. In his sketches for the helmets of the Scottish warriors can already easily be traced prototypes of the Teutonic knights of *Alexander Nevsky*, made a quarter of a century later.

The production was not a success as a whole. It only lasted a week, and then vanished from the repertory. With it ended the career of the Central Educational Theatre.

Eisenstein drew from this failure a justifiable conclusion about the indispensable unity of ideas in the direction and the design of a production. He said that he had had enough of working for directors who did not understand the ideas of painters; that sets and costumes, however interesting they may be, cannot save a production which is badly or mistakenly directed.

Already he was dreaming of his own theatre. For him the apprenticeship period was over. But before he could fully realize his ideas, we again combined to 'invent' a production which clearly and definitively confirmed his artistic positions.

Spring of 1922 remained memorable for us, not only because of the first contact with Shakespeare, but also because we witnessed Meyerhold's rehearsals for *The Magnanimous Cuckold*, by Crommelynck. Everyone who saw this production has retained the memory of one of the most controversial and at the same time one of the most brilliant of theatrical productions. The rehearsals were outstandingly interesting. Meyerhold was in top form. Every rehearsal was a sort of private production. As I have already said, Meyerhold demonstrated their playing to the actors in an altogether astonishing way. In this case he took the part of every actor, male or female. His genius for improvisation was extended to the full. His ungainly figure was now on the stage, among Popova's constructivist décors, now in the auditorium. His well-known exclamation of 'Fine!' acted like a whip to the actors, who worked with an ardour of inspiration.

Eisenstein and myself attended the triumphant première of *Cuckold*; then left for Leningrad for the summer. There Foregger's Theatre was appearing on tour (actually in the Aquarium, where later Lenfilm Studios were to be installed). I took my friends Kozintsev and Trauberg to these performances and introduced them to Eisenstein. The principles of the Eccentric Theatre were naturally sympathetic to him, and Eisenstein's name figured on the list of future professors on the first poster for FEKS. But it was clear that we could not all four of us mount a production. Hence we divided the spheres of influence between us. Kozintsev and Trauberg stayed to 'conquer' Leningrad. Eisenstein and I decided to continue working with Foregger in Moscow. Having learnt our lesson from earlier bitter experience, we wanted this time not only to present our own scheme for sets and production, but also to write a play in which we could carry to their full extent the principles of theatrical art dearest to our hearts.

We had settled on the pantomime by Donani, *The Scarf of Columbine*. Meyerhold had produced it in collaboration with the painter Sapunov, and Tairov had revived it in his Kamerny Theatre under the title of *The Veil of Pierrette*. We had not of course seen Meyerhold's version, which dated back to 1912. As to Tairov's version, it seemed to us archaic and tasteless. We decided according to the conceptions of those times to 'urbanize' and 'actualize' it.

The first act, Pierrot's attic, was constructed *vertically*: that is to say that the immense window, occupying the entire scene area, was at the same time the stage. The characters had to move in vertical lines, clinging to the bars. The second act, in Harlequin's house, was to be accompanied by jazz, which was then a very great novelty; and the dancing master was no longer a human being, but an automaton, quite clearly conceived under the influence of Picasso's costumes for Cocteau's *Parade*. Eisenstein's idea was for Harlequin to appear on the stage from the auditorium, on a wire like a rope-walker. He later used the idea in his production of *Enough Simplicity in Every Wise Man*. . . .

After two months' work we had written the scenario for the pantomime, noting the smallest details – not only the plans for the production, but even every actor's every gesture, every lighting change, every trick. We had called our opus *The Garter of Columbine*. The first page carried a dedication: 'To Vsevolod Meyerhold, master of the scarf; from the apprentices of the garter.' All that remained was to define a term capable of encompassing all the principles of the accomplished work. Chance helped us.

At that time our favourite distraction was the American Mountains in the House of the People (foreigners call them 'the Russian Mountains').* You might well say that all the theories of Eccentricism were born on these American Mountains. One day after one of these 'excursions' I arrived at Eisenstein's home so excited and worked up that he asked me what was the

---

* Though the English call it 'the switchback'.

matter. I told him that I had just had ten turns on my favourite fairground attraction. Then he exclaimed: 'Listen! That's an idea! Why not call our work "scenic attraction"? After all we want to shock the spectators with much the same physical effect as the attraction does.' And on the cover of *The Garter of Columbine*, above the dedication, he put: 'Invention of scenic attractions by Sergei Eisenstein and Sergei Yutkevitch.'

Subsequently Eisenstein changed the term to 'montage of attractions'.

Returning to Moscow in the autumn, we handed our scenario to Foregger, who included it in the plan of his repertory.

We impatiently awaited the realization of our project, but Foregger was in no hurry to present it. Soon, disappointed by Foregger, Eisenstein became assistant to Meyerhold, who was producing *The Death of Tarelkin*, by Sukhovo-Kobylin. Eisenstein's departure from 'Mastfor' was not accidental: by this time Foregger had abandoned his researches into new forms of a political propagandist theatre. He was vacillating between pure stylization and a purely distractional entertainment of the music-hall type, in keeping with the tastes of NEP audiences. I continued to work for a time at 'Mastfor' as a designer, and tried my hand at direction: in the production *Parade of Charlatans*, which consisted of medieval French comedies, I mounted one of the farces of Tabarin. Towards the end of the 1922–3 season, along with Vladimir Mass and a whole group of actors, I left the theatre in demonstration against its drift.

At this point I should say that outside our infatuation with the eccentric theatre, circus and music-hall, the cinema bit by bit came to enter our lives. The Civil War had ended, and little by little the first foreign films began to penetrate the blockade. Also Dziga Vertov made his appearance, with his first *Kino-Pravdas*.

At the beginning of 1923 Eisenstein headed the Peretru group, the workers' touring company of Proletcult [the name Peretru, which comprises an obscure pun, is an abbreviation of Peredvnaia (Rabochaia) Truppa]. Six months later, with this company, Eisenstein mounted his first production, Ostrovsky's *Enough Simplicity in Every Wise Man*, in which he included, among other attractions, the cinema. It was thus that he made his first short film, a parody of imported adventure pictures.* This production, presented in the spring of 1923, can be considered as the starting-point of Eisenstein's real career. His name was soon to sound throughout the world: it remains for ever the proper pride of Soviet culture.

How I Became A Film-maker

In F. Anstey's novel *The Brass Bottle*, the hero, having rashly broken the seal upon an ancient vase which he has bought at an auction sale, finds himself face to face with a genie who has been imprisoned therein for thousands of years. The genie, gifted with the power to do the most extraordinary miracles,

---

* But it was also a parody of Dziga Vertov's *Kino-Pravda*.

at once decides to show his gratitude; and in so doing causes the hero endless embarrassments and troubles. . . .

I experienced the feelings of a simple mortal who has liberated magic powers which are beyond his control, on the memorable, icy morning of the winter of 1924, when I found myself for the first time alone with a camera. It was in the Mejrabpom-Russ studios, which were then in the Petrovsky Park.

The camera which I had to tame belonged to that breed of antediluvian monsters with the aid of which Georges Méliès had made his magic films. In front of the ancient Pathé, on the plywood stage, writhed a pile of snakes from the zoological gardens. The young actor, who had never been in a film before and who, as the hero, was to be thrown with his hands tied into the snake-pit, kept his distance, anxiously looking now at me and now at the heap of harmless adders whom a melancholy zoo-keeper stirred with the end of a stick. The electricians, perched on their equipment, were waiting for the director's orders, but I was incapable of uttering a single word.

Elsewhere on the other half of our stage, the young assistant Raizman was energetically shouting orders, preparing the shooting of some Mejrabpom superproduction. I looked at him with anguish and envy. It seemed quite plain that he knew all the secrets of the movie kitchen! Everything was activity and lights; and all bathed in that mystery which has so powerful an effect on the uninitiated, plunged for the first time in the magical atmosphere of a studio.

But here in this sort of backroom where my unit was installed, all was depression and despair. . . .

A month earlier I had exchanged my peaceful profession of painter and stage director for the 'laurels' of an assistant director of cinema. The Moscow branch of Sevzapkino had decided to make a short comedy, *Give Us Radio!* For this they had hired someone who had happened along, claiming to be a pupil of Reinhardt and Lubitsch. This director turned out to be an illiterate imposter, as was revealed from the very start of shooting. He was thrown out, but the film had to be finished.

Hence it was that I enjoyed quite unexpected promotion, and found myself at this particular moment having to film, without help, a parody of the American adventure movies then in fashion. I was twenty, with no experience of the cinema; and perhaps my life would have turned out quite differently if, after the first painful hesitations, I had cancelled the shooting and, taking to my heels, left the studio once and for all.

But at this moment one of the oldest Russian producers, the painter Kozlovsky, approached me. He knew of me from my work in the theatre; and as he was an extremely kind and friendly man, he whispered a few words in my ear.

Precisely what the sympathetic Sergei Vassilivich said to me I do not recall. But the general sense was: 'Don't worry! We've all been through this.' His words gave me courage. I shouted the sacramental 'Ready to go!' which launched the usual studio chaos and . . . thus I became a director.

Give Us Radio! (Yutkevitch, 1925)

The first master who really initiated me into all the mysteries of the profession was the director Abram Room. In 1926 he invited me to be designer and assistant on his films *The Traitor* and *Bed and Sofa*. At this time the First State Cinema Factory was on Jitnaya Street. And though such films as *The Battleship Potemkin* and *The Death Ray* had been made in its little second-floor studio, the shooting units were very few and working at high pressure.

Thus it was that – thanks to fate – I became the general factotum in Room's unit. As painter, I built the sets; as assistant, I helped the director on the set and in the cutting-room; I prepared the set-ups, dressed the actors, saw to the props. As I refused no work and no problem, but plunged enthusiastically into the most obscure and most menial aspects of the hurly-burly of the business, two films were enough to instil in me a solid professional training.

My other godfather in the cinema was the old producer (now, alas, dead) A. V. Donachevsky. Long before, in his youth, he had emigrated to America to escape the persecution of the Tsarist Government. And he, without any intention of going into the cinema, was enrolled into the profession by the great D. W. Griffith. Returning home after the Revolution, this white-haired enthusiast set himself to build Soviet cinematography. He was director of production at the First State Cinema Factory and when I had passed the test of two films, he was the first to recommend entrusting me to work on my own.

Set design by Yutkevitch for *The Traitor*

Lace (Yutkevitch, 1928) and (below) *Give Us Radio!*

Lace

The Golden Mountains (Yutkevitch, 1931)

Donachevsky took the chance: he commissioned me to make a film. Thus it was that in 1927 I directed my first film, *Lace*, which was about the life of the komsomols.

Acquiring the secrets of the craft of film-making was not such a very complicated process. It was much more difficult to master all the secrets of the *art* of film-making. Practice showed that the film, exposed and edited according to all the technical laws, could not reveal itself of its own accord as a true work of great art. And it was at this moment that it became clear that the years of determined and intensive study, in studios and on the stage, had not been in vain. Absolutely the contrary: all that the theatre and painting had taught me was to provide the most solid possible foundation upon which to build a life in the cinema.

It is no accident that most of the film-makers of the 'first contingent' came from painting to films. We were all of us enthralled by the possibilities of the cinema, which permitted us to transform a film into a series of innumerable compositions, studied and frequently 'distorting', because, voluntarily or not, they denatured reality.

Painting was a great help at the start of my cinema career. It still helps me, though now it begins to restrict me when it becomes the *only* support, the only impulse and stimulus to cinema creation. In my first film, *Lace*, I remember that I was incapable of working out the form of a scene before seeing it in its pictorial composition. Later the process of the search for essence

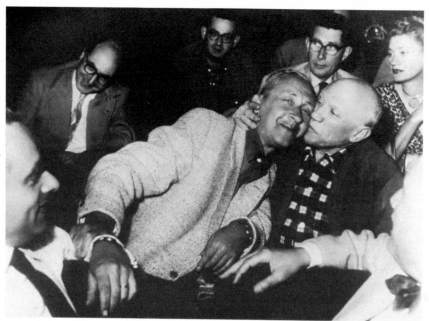

Yutkevitch and Picasso (*c.* 1956)

and for form acquired more and more unity and, thus, the solutions arrived at became more exact.

Nowhere is there so much search for a philosopher's stone, so much quasi-medieval scholasticism as in the problems of cinema theory. Working as they were in a new art, the artists and innovators really needed to recognize and establish its specific quality. In its time it was montage which was named the philosopher's stone of the cinema, and it was furiously defended, as much in theory as in practice, as the major element in the specificity of the new art. In the beginning this was a healthy and progressive phenomenon, but in subsequent stages of the evolution of the Soviet cinema the theory of the 'priority of montage' became a dead weight which hampered the forward progress of the cinema.

When it was a matter of cleaning out the Augean stables of the cinema, when it was vital to get rid of the Khanzhonkov heritage, polemic violence was understandable, aimed as it was against all the theatricality, the cheap literary values (more simply, against all the trash) intensively implanted by a bourgeois culture. But when one moved on to constructive and positive work, it became clear that the problem of 'pure cinema' was infinitely more complex than it seemed to its fanatics. What was the use of making a 'revolution' only if in practice you were to come back to imitations of American police films (*The Death Ray*), borrowing everything from the genre – everything, that is, except its essential and obligatory trait: the distractive interest?

The General Line (Eisenstein and Alexandrov, 1929)

So ended the first sterile phase of the search for a philosopher's stone, and so was born the first 'homunculus' of the cinema.

Yet the work was not in vain. On the earth that had been cleared, two films very soon appeared which were to determine the style of a true Soviet cinema. They were Eisenstein's films *Strike* and *The Battleship Potemkin*.

Employing all the expressive power of montage, Eisenstein in no respect took the road of imitating American models. The enormous importance of *Strike* – still to my mind insufficiently appreciated – lay in this: for the first time the image of the worker made its appearance on the screen. For the first time the triumphant story of the revolutionary struggle of the working class was shown by a Soviet artist with an enormous persuasive force. And this struggle proved a thousand times more exciting than hundreds of 'sensational' German or American pictures. *Strike*, and *Potemkin* after it, were ideal examples of truly innovatory works.

But the innovatory qualities in them, it seems to me, were not the result of preconceived formulas. They were really the result of the imperative demands of the theme itself – a theme without precedence in art and which, consequently, necessitated forms that were without precedent. The idea, the theme, the story matter thus brought forth the form. But we all know, too, that that form which comes from the thought and the emotion of the artist is in correlation with the content, and that they reciprocally influence each the other.

The General Line

Eisenstein's theory of 'montage of attractions', born in a quite different field of activity, clearly found here its reflection and its application; but I am sure that it was not this which played the determining role in the success of these films. In *Strike* you still find the tricks of his laboratory experiments which, often, are in contradiction to the truly realist material of the film. But *The Battleship Potemkin* is one of the most complete and pure works of cinematography – not just in the Soviet film, but in the whole of international cinema. I can think of only one other like it: Dovzhenko's *Earth*.

At the First Congress of Soviet Workers, Leonid Sobolev said, admirably: 'The Party and the Government have given everything to the Soviet writer. They have taken from him only one right: the right to write badly.'

My country has given me everything. Trusting in me, it has given me the right to work for 'the most important of all the arts'.

In our country the cinema is deprived of only one right: the right to be stupid and irresponsible, the right to be a money-making machine, the right to be a carnival attraction.

In our country the cinema has the obligation to be intelligent, profound, responsible towards the people.

We have a vast and wonderful responsibility.

Sketches by Eisenstein

2. Sergei Mikhailovitch Eisenstein

The title chosen by Eisenstein for the first of these essays is in fact the title of a once well-known German sex education book. It appears over several autobiographical essays, and may well have been intended ultimately for an unrealized volume of memoirs. In any event it is especially suited to this essay, in which Eisenstein compares his actual father's evasiveness over imparting biological 'mysteries' to his son, with his spiritual father's – Meyerhold's – equal evasiveness in the matter of artistic 'mysteries'.

Despite the qualifications in respect of Meyerhold's private character (which carry little conviction), Eisenstein's avowal of adulation for his Master is all the more remarkable since it was written in 1946, barely six years after Meyerhold's execution, and at a time when his name was utterly erased from the record of Soviet art. It is perhaps ungrateful to regret that Eisenstein does not describe more specifically the experience of working with Meyerhold on the Actor's Theatre production of *A Doll's House* (20 April 1922). Edward Braun (in *Meyerhold on Theatre*) says of the production that it 'caused a scandal. It was rushed on after five rehearsals and performed against a background of flats taken straight from stock and propped back to front against stage walls, symbolizing – or so Meyerhold claimed – "the bourgeois milieu against which Nora rebels". This was more than the "Nezlobittsy" could stand and they fled after the one production, leaving Meyerhold and his company as sole tenants of the dilapidated theatre which they were to occupy until it closed for renovation in 1932.'

Eisenstein was born in Riga, 23 January 1898, and studied at the Institute of Civil Engineering in Petrograd. After service in the Red Army he became a pupil of Meyerhold and designed settings for Foregger's Theatre, as Yutkevitch describes in the preceding article. From 1920 he worked at the Proletkult Theatre, and it was in one of his productions – as he describes in the second article that is included here – that he first tried his hand at film-making, with a short insert included in the play *Enough Simplicity in Every Wise Man*.

In 1924 Eisenstein made his first full-length film, *Strike*, in which may still be seen evidences of his theatrical experiences, but which was in every respect revolutionary, especially by its introduction onto the screen, for the first time, of the mass hero. His next film *The Battleship Potemkin* (1925), quoted frequently by the other authors of this book, was still, in 1958, voted the Best Film of All Time by the international jury at the Brussels Universal and International Exhibition. Following *October* (1927) and *The General Line* (1929), Eisenstein, along with Alexandrov and Tissé, embarked on an extended tour of Europe and America, where they were commissioned to prepare a film for Paramount. Two scripts – *Sutter's Gold* and *An American Tragedy* – were written, but all projects proved abortive and the trio moved on to Mexico to make a film produced by Upton Sinclair. Disagreement with Sinclair prevented Eisenstein from completing *Qué Viva Mexico!* and in 1931 Eisenstein and his collaborators returned home. The greater part of Eisenstein's creative energy during the remaining years of his life was necessarily given over to writing and to teaching (transcriptions of his classes at the State Institute of Cinematography reveal him to have been an outstanding teacher).

Two versions of *Bezhin Meadow* were begun and abandoned during 1935–6, and all the material shot was lost during the war. (An assembly of stills from the film was issued as a short film, under the signature of Sergei Yutkevitch, in 1967.) Not until 1938 did Eisenstein complete a sound film, *Alexander Nevsky*, with a score by Prokoviev. Prokoviev also wrote the musical score for *Ivan the Terrible* (1941–6), an intended three-part film which was halted after criticism of the second part. This second part was only released in 1958, ten years after the death of Eisenstein on 11 February 1948.

Eisenstein's importance and influence is out of all proportion to the actual bulk of his *œuvre* – only six completed films over a period of twenty-five years. The vast culture and intelligence he brought to film-making, the intellectual and expressive possibilities revealed by *Strike* and *Potemkin*, established him as one of the incontestable great masters of the art of the cinema.

44

'Wie sag' ich's meinem Kind?'
and My First Film

'Wie sag' ich's meinem Kind?'

As well as a physical father, there always appears upon the roads and ways of life, a spiritual father.

It pleased the Lord that when it came to the question of 'secrets' my spiritual father was very much the same sort of man as my physical father.

Mikhail Osipovitch* was infinitely evasive when it came to questions about biological 'secrets'.

Vsevolod Emilievitch† was still more evasive when it was a question of the 'secrets' of the art of direction.

By strict biblical code, it is perhaps rather dreadful to admit that I did not much care for Mikhail Osipovitch. . . .

In any event it was natural for me to give all my affection to my second father.

It must be said that never did I love, adore, idolize anyone as I did my master.

Will someone among my own students some day say this about me?

No, he will not. And that is no reflection on me and my pupils, but indicates the relation between me and my master.

---

* M. O. Eisenstein, the father of Eisenstein.

† V. E. Meyerhold.

For I am unworthy to loosen his sandals – and besides, he wore felt boots in the unheated studios of Novinski Boulevard.

And even when I am a very old man I will still consider myself unworthy to kiss the dust of his footsteps, even though his errors as a man have perhaps effaced from the pages of our theatrical art all traces of the steps of one of the greatest masters of the theatre.

It is not possible to live without loving, without deifying, without passion and adoration.

He was a stupefying man. The living refutation of the idea that 'genius and evildoing are incompatible things'.

What good fortune to know this magician and sorcerer of the theatre!

What ill luck to depend upon the man!

What good fortune to be able to learn by watching him!

What ill luck to come trustingly to him to ask a question!

In my innocence I long ago asked him a whole series of questions about hidden difficulties.

His eagle face with its piercing eyes, the devastating curl of the lips beneath the rapacious, arched nose, suddenly took on the look of Mikhail Osipovitch.

A glassy look, then fleeting, then becoming infinitely remote, then official and polite, then almost sympathetic and mocking, then ironical, as if surprised: 'Now tell me. . . . How curious! . . . Mmm-yes. . . .'

I can say with absolute precision where the expression 'to spit in someone's eye' arose!

This had no effect upon my love and adoration.

It was just that my soul filled with a great sadness.

I was not very lucky with my fathers. . . .

His lectures were like serpents' songs.

'He who hears these songs, forgets the whole world. . . .'

His lectures were mirages and dreams.

Feverishly one took notes.

And when one awoke, in the notebook there remained only a 'devil knows what.'*

What Meyerhold said it is impossible to remember.

Perfumes, sounds, colours.

Golden mist over everything.

Untouchable.

Impalpable.

Mystery upon mystery.

Veil after veil.

Not seven veils.

But eight, twelve, thirty, half a hundred.

Evoking all kinds of suggestions, they flew in the hands of the magician, enwrapping the mysteries.

---

* Reference to a phrase in Gogol.

It is strange indeed.

The magician seems to have things upside down.

The romantic 'Me' is bewitched, absorbed, listens.

The rationalist 'Me' grumbles and is deaf.

'When are the mysteries to be unveiled? When shall we get on to methodology? When will this inside-out striptease come to an end?'

A winter of delightful intoxication passed, leaving in our hands: nothing. But then:

The First RSFSR Theatre combines with the Nezlobin Theatre.

Who does not work, does not eat.

And in the theatre, he does not eat who does not play (at least it was like this in 1921!).

And now, with three rehearsals *A Doll's House* will be presented.

Sometimes I asked myself: is it that Meyerhold simply cannot communicate and reveal the mysteries?

Because he cannot himself see and formulate.

Be that as may, though the mystery had remained concealed through the autumn and winter, in the spring our hands and feet would be untied.

In the course of working it is impossible not to reveal oneself completely.

In the course of working, it is impossible to deceive.

In the course of working, there is not time to weave the invisible spider webs, the golden stuff of the imagination, trailing in dream. In the course of working you have to *do*.

And all that which for two terms had been cautiously and viciously concealed was revealed, triumphantly, in three days of rehearsals.

I have seen quite a few people and things in my time. . . .

But nothing will ever efface in my memory the impressions of those three days of rehearsals of *A Doll's House* in the gym on Novinski Boulevard.

I remember my constant trembling.

It was not cold, but excitement, nerves stretched to their limit.

There were bars all around the walls of the gymnasium.

And for one whole day, to the curt commands of Ludmilla Gyetye, we conscientiously disjointed our limbs.

Even now I have feet which can disjoint themselves, and at forty-eight I can still surprise dancers by my impeccable *levé du pied*.

Squatting between the bar and the wall, holding my breath, my back to the window, I gaze steadily in front of me.

And from that perhaps arises my second tendency:

To dig, to dig, to dig.

To enter, penetrate, bury myself in every crack in the problem, seeming to go always deeper and deeper and to come nearer to the core of it.

There is no assistance to be sought from anywhere else.

Except not to hide what has been found: to bring it into the daylight – in lessons, in printing, in articles, in books.

And by the way . . . do you know the surest means of concealment? It is to reveal all, right to the very last veil!

My First Film

In Ostrovsky's play *Enough Simplicity in Every Wise Man*, one of the plot motives is the diary in which Glumov records all his adventures.

In approaching the problems of a revolutionary 'modernization' of Ostrovski, that is to say in effecting the social transformation of the characters into their present-day equivalents (Kroutitzky-Joffre, Mamaev-Milukov, etc., up to Golutvin who nowadays would be a NEP-man*) we likewise modernized the diary.

The diary was replaced by *Kino-Pravda* which at that time was just becoming popular.

The complex theme of the psychological play of the adventurer who adapts himself to the very different people that he meets, was interpreted by us in the eccentric manner, by means of conventional changes of costume on stage. In the newsreel this was carried further. By a perilous leap Glumov changes himself into whatever object is desirable for each particular person.

Thus he is transformed into a machine-gun in front of Joffre-Kroutitzky who is ensconced, wearing a clown's costume, on a tank in the courtyard of the War Academy. Joffre was played by Antonov, who was later, in the role of Vakulintchuk, to incite the uprising in *Potemkin*.

Faced with another clown, Milukov-Mamaev, smitten by sententious sermons, Glumov changes into an ass from the zoo. Finally, faced with the aunt, consumed by passion for her young nephews, he is transformed into a baby Inkidjinov, anticipating by five years the appearance of his father on the screen – as the hero of *Storm Over Asia*!

Nowadays it seems utterly crazy, but in 1923 my request to shoot these scenes out of doors provoked great panic. For some reason it was considered extremely complicated. They insisted urgently on the indispensability of a black velvet backdrop and so on. Even the cameraman Lemberg, not wishing to risk the adventure, refused to shoot it.

In the end it was Frantzisson who made it with me. And as the people at Goskino thought I might misbehave too much, they assigned to me as instructor . . . Dziga Vertov! . . .

Anyway, after two or three sequences had been shot, Dziga Vertov abandoned us to our fate.

In all we shot 120 metres in one day. I remember very well – it was Thursday and the première of *Enough Simplicity* was on the Saturday. . . . It was one of the first unions of theatre and cinema, along with FEKS' *Marriage* and Gardin's *Iron Heel*. It was in fact an essay in what was later to serve Erwin Piscator for his brilliant and fugitive work in Germany.

These shots had nothing to do with cinema properly called, although close-ups were mixed with pans and even a fragment of adventure film, with

---

* A new-rich of the NEP period.

Alexandrov in a black mask, cloak and top hat, clambering up roofs and leaping from an 'aeroplane' into a car travelling at full speed. The car arrived at the entrance of the Proletkult Theatre at the very moment that the film ended on the screen; and Alexandrov, yelling, burst into the hall holding the reel of film in his hand.

Under the title of *Proletkult's Spring Smiles* this little bit of film was later included in *Spring Kino-Pravda*, shown on 12 May 1923 for the anniversary of *Kino-Pravda*.

What is odd is that, even at that time, after having calculated the length of our film in advance with a stop-watch – 8 metres – we deviated ever so slightly from the planned length, and shot . . . 120 metres.

It must be believed that certain characteristic aspects of our creative work are revealed from the first 'smiles'.*

---

* A single short episode from the projected film *1905* grew into *Potemkin*, in 1925.

Strike (Eisenstein, 1925)

3. Grigori Vassilievitch Alexandrov

In this interview, recorded in Moscow in July 1965, Grigori Alexandrov recalls his collaboration with Eisenstein, which extended from 1921 when Alexandrov was recruited as an actor for an Eisenstein production at Proletkult, until the return of Eisenstein, Alexandrov and Tisse from Mexico in 1931.

Born in 1903, Alexandrov began his working life as a wardrobe assistant, scene-painter and electrician at the Opera House at Ekaterinburg (now Sverdlovsk). In 1918 he enrolled in the production course of the Workers' and Peasants' Theatre; and in 1921 arrived in Moscow to become an actor at the First Proletkult Theatre. Alexandrov acted the main role in Eisenstein's first attempt at film-making, *Glumov's Diary*, went on to be actor and assistant director on *Strike* (1924) and *Potemkin* (1925); and was credited as co-writer and co-director on *October* (1927) and *The General Line* (1929). He was associated with Eisenstein and Pudovkin on the famous manifesto on sound films; then accompanied Eisenstein and Tisse on their tour of Europe and America. In Paris Alexandrov directed *Romance Sentimentale*, an experimental sound short; in America he worked with Eisenstein and Ivor Montagu on the two Paramount scripts; and in Mexico he collaborated on *Qué Viva Mexico!*

Of Alexandrov's own films, made since 1933, the most successful have been his musical comedies, notably *Jazz Comedy* (1934), *Circus* (1936) and *Volga-Volga* (1938), his favourite musical star in these being his wife, Lyuba Orlova. Since then Alexandrov has made *Parade of Athletes* (1938), *Bright Road* (1940), *Film Notes on Battle No. 4* (1941), *Springtime* (1947), *Meeting on the Elbe* (1949), *Glinka* (1952), *From Man to Man* (1958), *Russian Souvenir* (1960), *Lenin in Switzerland* (1966). In addition to these films Alexandrov made a two-reel documentary, *Internationale*, to commemorate the fifteenth anniversary of the 1917 Revolution, in 1932; and wrote scenarios for V. Cherviakov's *The Girl from the Far River* (1928) and for the Vassiliev Brothers' *The Sleeping Beauty* (1930).

Working with Eisenstein

It was in 1921 that I first met Sergei Eisenstein. At that time he was a painter, and was doing the décors for Jack London's *The Mexican* for the First Workers' Proletcult Theatre. I was an actor in the play, playing first a journalist, then an American boxer. The production was directed by an artist of the Moscow Art Theatre, Smichliayev. Eisenstein and I decided to organize our own theatre, a theatre which would perform in the squares and the streets. We were agreed that artificial décors were a thing of the past. We started to form our own troupe; we collected eighteen youngsters and Eisenstein became our director.

We started off with a production which Eisenstein conceived upon a well-known Ostrovski play, *Enough Simplicity in Every Wise Man*. We decided to have a circular carpet made, like a circus ring, to spread it out in a square and to perform on it for the passers-by. But as we rehearsed we felt the need of props. Then we wanted to introduce acrobatic numbers: I walked on a tightrope and performed on the flying trapeze. At that time I belonged to a circus act, the Rudenko Brothers, and we called ourselves 'The Eagles of the Ural Mountains'. Eisenstein decided to use our acrobatic skills. And as the production took shape it became more and more elaborate, the amount of material increased, we needed trapezes and tightropes, and the problem of transferring from place to place became more and more complicated. We therefore decided to perform first in Moscow, in a building on the site of the present House of Friendship. They allocated us this hall, in which we installed temporary seating just before we opened. The performances were a big success, but we never played it anywhere else.

We decided to present the next production in a gas factory. The writer Sergei Tretyakov, internationally known as the author of *Roar, China!*, wrote a play called *Gas Masks* on the theme of a conflict between the management of the factory and the workers, culminating in the explosion of the gas machines. Eisenstein decided that a dusty hall would not do for the theatre, and we found in the Moscow gas-works a workshop of which one half was filled with machinery and the other half was empty. So instead of building décors, we installed the seats so that the audience faced real machinery which would perform its own and actual role in the play. In this production I played an old woman. We were then eccentric youngsters and we invented methods which were quite improbable. Our production was designed so that at the end of the performance actual workmen came up to the machines and opened the valves: the flames that were lit served to illustrate the idea that these machines, in accordance with the theme of the play, had been repaired.

Unfortunately this production was not a great success, because the public had certain habits, and were more ready to turn up at a theatre than at a factory to see a play. But by now it was altogether too complicated an operation for us to return to the traditional theatre. Moreover we had decided to use the cinema. As one of the Proletcult productions figured this same *Enough Simplicity* . . . and we decided to introduce film episodes into it. I played Golutvin. At that time Harry Piel was extremely popular on the screen – the James Bond of his period – and Eisenstein made me a kind of Harry Piel. In silk hat and evening dress I leapt from an aeroplane into a moving car, without any trick work I might add, and clambered over quite impossible rooftops. I stole the diary belonging to the hero of the play, which provided the motive for our chases. Now this diary was recorded on celluloid: it was our first film. . . . This film ran about twenty minutes and was included by Dziga Vertov in his montage *Kino-Pravda's Spring Smiles* as an example of the avant-garde in the art of the theatre. It was the début of our cinema careers.

In this film insert there were primarily circus turns and eccentric sequences. And after it was finished, Eisenstein wanted to continue working in the cinema. I was his assistant and we began to write a scenario on the history of the Russian Revolution. Initially we thought of doing a series of episodes from 1905 to the October Revolution. But then we were taken by the theme of *Strike*. The whole team who worked with Eisenstein in his little theatre played the principal roles. I was still his assistant, and I played the part of the factory foreman. I seemed always to have the job of being the traitor in Eisenstein's films; in *Potemkin*, for instance, I played the officer Guiliarovsky who shoots the mutineers and is later thrown overboard.

Strike was an avant-garde film because at that time the traditions of the

Tissé, Eisenstein and Alexandrov during the shooting of *Strike*

old cinema were still strong and the eternal triangle situation was the norm. We worked hard to show through the medium of the cinema certain new aspects of life; and this led Eisenstein to the conviction that the individual hero no longer had any place, and must be replaced by the mass hero, the worker masses. Of course, when the film came out it provoked great controversy, since it was in direct contradiction to everything that was going on around us on the screens. All the same it was the first step towards success.

The idea of the 'montage of attractions' came to Eisenstein from productions mounted by us in the First Workers' Theatre. Having, as I have said, taken a very classic play by Ostrovski which described realistically the daily life of Muscovite merchants, Eisenstein turned it into an eccentric spectacle, with acrobatic turns, clowns and musical interludes. Even the title of the play was printed on the posters in such a way that in its original Russian form the words 'A LITTLE . . . OF . . . EVERYTHING' stood out.

Moving on from this experiment, and also from the success of the production, Eisenstein wished to elaborate a theory of the montage of attractions, because he was persuaded that what counts for the audience is the impression, the effect, not so much the psychological justification of the action, not so much its logic as the *effect*, which he wanted to obtain by means of montage. But it must be said here that with Eisenstein theory and practice were quite different things. He often gave free rein to his imagination to invent theories but, in practice, he did not carry them out. In practical work he was much more cautious. His theories were conceived with an eye to a cinema yet to be. He realized that the public would not accept at the outset his theoretical researches and he made his films with the aim of reaching the audience. His theoretical ideas and his imaginary inventions were applied only bit by bit and progressively.

Today a curious thing is happening, for people are doing things which while they are not a repetition of our researches are nevertheless an echo of them. The progress of life often follows a rising spiral: what is happening today is rather close to this past, but reaches higher and further. The current spiral is passing directly above the one which represents our revolutionary experiments and it seems that these have returned to fashion in literature, theatre and, most recently, in the cinema.

Next we were commissioned to make a film for the anniversary of 1905. The year 1925 was close – the twentieth anniversary of the first Russian Revolution. The original idea was a vast scenario, the whole story of the Revolution, but time was short, we had to make a film quickly and we took Nina Ferdinandovna Agadjanova's scenario, which was the basis of the film, to Odessa. There we saw the famous steps and various other natural décors, and we decided to take a single episode from this vast scenario in order to be able to finish the film in time for the anniversary of the Revolution. So we made *The Battleship Potemkin*. Eisenstein was twenty-five and I was nineteen.

We wrote numerous episodes of the scenario; but as we went along, meeting people and learning new details, we changed everything. I recall one particular instance. We were in Odessa, unable to work because of thick fog. Then Eisenstein, Tissé and myself hired a boat and went out into the harbour. Momentarily the fog would lift, giving glimpses of beautiful misty landscapes. We decided to shoot, without knowing exactly what we were going to get. We filmed the mists; and in the evening when we got back to our hotel we composed the 'requiem' on the death of Vakulintchuk which was later to become famous. We improvised the film as we worked. I think that that quality – the possibility for the director-author to use the material around him in the course of shooting, not according to a pre-established scenario, but snatching anything of value which presents itself – is lost today: nowadays we work too much in offices, round a table, writing in advance. It seems to me that the qualities of *The Battleship Potemkin* depend to a great extent on this vital perception of reality on the move.

At this point comes our famous 'manifesto' on the sound film. In 1927 we heard about the experiments which were going on in this field. We were very friendly with Pudovkin, and met frequently to muse over what would happen to the cinema the day sound came to stay. We spent innumerable evenings in these discussions. When we learned what the first sound films were, and about their form and content, we decided to formulate in writing our reflections on the future of this new art form. It was in 1928 that Eisenstein and Pudovkin asked me to draw up the substance of our conversations. I wrote a few pages, and we finished the preparation collectively, adding new points. We did a lot of work on it and all our various drafts are preserved in the State archives. But later, after other sound films had come out abroad, we decided to publish a declaration which has subsequently been called a 'manifesto' and in which we wanted to state the idea that all that the silent cinema had acquired was threatened by the appearance of sound. Because the most simple and the most facile method would be the application of theatrical experience. This would be not sound film, but talking film, for instead of expressing everything by the specific means of the cinematographic art, people would prefer simply to *say*! This would not, from our point of view, be as interesting as the sound film might be.

At that time we were very young, very 'Left' in our artistic researches, and in this manifesto we expressed, perhaps not very profoundly, what we were saying elsewhere. We wanted to express all this in an effective way. Whether we succeeded or not, we stated in this text that the sound film would pass through quite a long period in which cinematographic art would be weakened, and would cease to use its own specific means of expression; that literary and theatrical methods would usurp the cinema. And in fact this is just what happened: predictably the rich experience of theatre and literature predominated, submerging properly cinematographic means. Today some directors strive to reverse the tendency, and we ourselves, in *Qué Viva Mexico!* wished to realize in practice what we had formulated theoretically in our manifesto. Unfortunately, as you know well enough, it was not possible. Later, when Eisenstein came to make *Alexander Nevsky* and *Ivan the Terrible* he could not bring himself to apply the principles of the manifesto in his films: he preferred a more conventional form, based on the experience of theatrical art. But I feel that many of the avant-garde methods now used by young directors, employed for example in *L'Année Dernière à Marienbad*, were already expounded in our manifesto.

I think that this manifesto still has a role to play in the evolution of the sound cinema. Its fundamental thought was that all the elements of the cinema – image, sound, colour, music – ought not to be simply illustrations of the atmosphere and the ideas, simply there for emphasis, but that they are the elements of a composition, and that the true cinema will be born when each of these elements no longer illustrates the dramatic action, but becomes an independent theme, playing its own role, as in a symphony. I feel that we were too hurried in publishing this manifesto, and that many things were omitted from it. Now, in the collected works of Eisenstein, everyone can read a more profound analysis of these ideas; and it seems to me that although he has already left us, Eisenstein – along with Pudovkin – will again play a great role in the evolution of the cinema of the future.

In 1928 we were invited to Hollywood. On the way, in the autumn of 1929, we stopped in Berlin. There we helped a young German cinéaste by giving him a little advice on how to finish a film called *Asphyxiating. Gas*. Then, in Switzerland, where we went to take part in the famous La Sarraz congress,

October (Eisenstein and Alexandrov, 1928)

we were invited to make the first Swiss film, a documentary on abortion called *Le Bonheur et le Malheur des Femmes*. And when recently I was shooting my new film, *Lenin in Switzerland*, the Swiss cinéastes greeted me as the founder of their national cinema. Likewise I was in Mexico in 1956, and the 'junta' of Mexican directors organized a reception in my honour, in as much as I was the representative of that 'troika' – Eisenstein, Tissé and myself – who first discovered cinema in Mexico; they considered us the founders of the Mexican cinema and of the Mexican 'style'. So we are regarded as the founders of no less than three national cinemas – Soviet, Swiss and Mexican.

When we arrived in Paris in November 1929 we were very keen to learn the technique of sound film; and we decided to make a little experimental film which would serve as our apprenticeship. We crossed France in a motor-car: in Brittany we shot a storm at sea, in the Midi we shot magnolias in bloom – in fact we had no idea what our film was going to be; we were filming France. Back in Paris we took an old sentimental Russian romance and, using an experimental form of montage, we tried to make a film. But at that moment, Paramount insisted that Eisenstein should at last report to Hollywood. He went off with Tissé, leaving me to do the editing and mixing of *Romance Sentimentale* alone. I did it as quickly as I was able – in one month – so that I could join the rest of the team in Hollywood.

October

There we wrote several scenarios; Ivor Montagu worked with us as an assistant. We wrote a comedy, *The Glass House*, about a house whose walls were all transparent and which was therefore uninhabitable. It was a satire on the American way of life and the banks would not finance such a film. Then we thought up another scenario, *Sutter's Gold*, inspired by the life of the Swiss schoolteacher who had opened up California.* This scenario also seemed to be too revolutionary for Hollywood, and once again we were unable to begin shooting. These scenarios will be published in the sixth volume of Eisenstein's collected works, and I think they will prove very interesting.

At that point we were invited to Mexico by a group of friends from that country, including Diego Rivera. We spent seven months there filming *Qué Viva Mexico!* I think everyone knows the tragedy of that picture. Just when we were on the point of finishing shooting and there only remained two or three months' work on the film, Upton Sinclair, the American writer who was financing us, decided that his connection with our film might hurt his chances of being elected Governor of California. He therefore cut off our

---

* Based on Blaise Cendrars' novel *Gold*. The scenario, along with that for *An American Tragedy* is published in Ivor Montagu's *With Eisenstein in Hollywood*, Berlin, 1968. Montagu claims that no scenario for *The Glass House* was written.

Jazz Comedy (Alexandrov, 1934)

supplies. We could not find other means of finance and so decided to take what we had shot back to Moscow in order to edit the film there. The film was sent with our baggage, and got as far as Le Havre, where it was seized and sent back to the United States on the demand of Sinclair. Eisenstein quarrelled with Sinclair, who proposed that we should return to Hollywood to edit the film. Eisenstein refused and only went back to America to wind up our affairs; he had several meetings with Sinclair, but nothing came of them.

Since we are talking about that film, I would like to say that I would love to finish it one day. I think that its material has not dated at all, that it is not in any way dead, and that it would be of as much artistic as ideological interest. I feel that the situation is at this moment propitious for an agreement for the definitive completion of the film. The more so since I myself worked on the scenario and the shooting, since I have in my possession all the original material on Eisenstein's ideas, and since I frequently edited with him. Hence it would be easy for me to complete the film as he wanted it. I hope that one day we shall see the definitive version of the film, and I am sure that it will be successful, for it has much of that quality towards which the cinema of today is aiming, without achieving it as Eisenstein did. Many attempts, such as the *nouvelle vague*, can only go so far: they begin well, but they quickly come to an *impasse*. While in *Qué Viva Mexico!* are elaborated the

Jazz Comedy

principles of the synthetic use of image and sound, not of synchronous sound but of sound which, as I just now said, is in conflict with the image. Because Eisenstein believed that synchronous sound, agreeing with the image, is a theatrical means, while in the cinema sound must be an element of the composition: sometimes the conflict between sound and image produces quite new impressions. In the cinema it is possible to hear not only what someone says, but also what he thinks; and it can happen that he thinks things that are quite different from what he is saying; the cinema discovers the interior world of the person much better than one can understand it simply in listening to what he says. In this film we foresaw large uses of this technique.

For instance the director spoke with his characters. In the episode *La Soldadera*, when the wives of the Mexican soldiers are following their men, the *metteur en scène* asks one of them, 'Where are you going, woman?' She stops, turns to the camera and says, 'I don't know.' The *metteur en scène* continues. 'Think well where you are going. To the war. With the soldiers. You risk your life.' She answers, 'But I love him,' and follows after the soldier. This technique of the author carrying on a dialogue with one of his characters was something quite new. Today I see many of the things which were then sketched out used in certain new films, but, I fear, not with success.

Eisenstein with the crew for *October*

That is why I would like so much to materialize all this in order to show how far the thought of Eisenstein was ahead of his time.

When we got back from Mexico we began to make very different films. Everyone wanted to make comedies. Eisenstein had an idea for *M.M.M.* – *Maxim Maximovitch Maximov* – and Dovzhenko also wanted to do a comedy, *The Tsar*. I had begun to write the scenario of *Jazz Comedy*. For some reason they were unable to realize their projects, but I was launched on a series of musical comedies: *Jazz Comedy, Volga-Volga* and *Springtime*. At the same time I made several documentaries, and also historical films, such as *The Composer Glinka*, or dramatic films like *Meeting on the Elbe*. Currently I am working on a new film *Lenin in Switzerland*. Lenin, in exile from 1895 to 1917, spent more than eight years in Switzerland – a very interesting period of his life. . . .

After this I would like to undertake a re-editing of *October*, the film which Eisenstein and I did together – both the writing and the *mise en scène* – for the tenth anniversary of the October Revolution. Now that we are almost at the fiftieth anniversary* I would like to stand on its feet again a film that was pretty well knocked down at the time. It was very much cut and we were not

---

* 1967. Alexandrov has subsequently re-edited both *October* and *Potemkin*.

able to do it as we had wanted. Now it is possible to realize it just as we wanted – as Eisenstein wished it.

Another of my cherished projects, as I have already said, is to edit *Qué Viva Mexico!* Seventy-five thousand metres of negative which we shot in Mexico are preserved by the Museum of Modern Art Film Library in New York. The material has been used in several films: Marie Seton made one of them, and I think a dozen films have been made with various episodes. All of these films were very far from Eisenstein's ideas. The various scenarios so far published are different versions of these ideas, and do not include his final version. In 1956 it was agreed between Mr Richard Griffith of the Museum of Modern Art and myself that twelve Soviet films which the Film Library needed would be given in exchange for an integral copy of the *Qué Viva Mexico!* material. Unhappily the agreement has not been implemented owing to the deterioration of the political situation between our countries, but last year I resumed my correspondence with Mr Griffith and I hope to be able to realize my project to edit the film. In London in 1963 I was able to see four hours of rushes from the film, put together by the American historian Jay Leyda as study material. I took part in the showing in order to explain how we wanted to do the film, and I stayed on the platform from four in the afternoon until eleven at night. For nearly seven hours I was answering questions put by the English audience. I left that session convinced of the enormous interest that this film still excites today; and that is why it is my dearest wish to be able one day to give definitive form to it, as Eisenstein conceived it.

(Recorded in Moscow, 19 July 1965)

The Strange Adventures of Mr West in the Land of the Bolsheviks (Kuleshov, 1924)

4. Lev Vladimirovitch Kuleshov

Of the great Soviet directors of the first period, the name of Lev Kuleshov is perhaps least known in Britain, except to the most dedicated cinema enthusiasts. Yet his must be reckoned as one of the most significant influences in the whole development of film art. Among other distinctions he claims that over fifty per cent of Soviet directors since 1920 have been his pupils. The claim becomes all the more impressive when it is added that these pupils included Eisenstein and Pudovkin. In later years Pudovkin, through no fault of his own (he was always at pains to minimize his own role), constantly got credit for the discoveries and innovations of Kuleshov, his master.

Kuleshov was the first aesthetic theorist of the cinema. In 1917, when he was eighteen and had been only a few months at the Khanzhonkov Studios, he published his first articles in a film magazine. Seen against the background of a Russian cinema largely devoted to novelette themes, and lagging far behind the West in purely technical expertise and sophistication, the content of these precocious articles was startling. Two years before *Caligari* Kuleshov was defining, for instance, the key contribution of the designer in the expressive means of the cinema: 'The artist in the cinema paints with objects, walls and light. . . . It is almost unimportant what is in the shot. What is important is to dispose these objects and combine them for the purpose of their final single plane.'

Kuleshov made one film before the Revolution – *The Project of Engineer Prite* (1917). After the Revolution he was dispatched to the Eastern Front with a team of cameramen. Returning to Moscow he was fairly soon recruited to the teaching staff of the State Film School – the first such school in the world.

Perhaps because it was all too clear that Kuleshov regarded most of his colleagues as stuffy conservatives, he was given his own 'workshop'. Pudovkin remembered that: 'It was located in a former private mansion on a small Moscow side-street. I went there one evening soon after I heard about it. There was a strange odour about the place, a mixture of lilac, celluloid and burned wires. Someone was improvising at the piano.'

On this occasion Pudovkin did not stay, since both he and Kuleshov were sent off with film units to the Western Front, where the Poles had launched a fresh attack. Kuleshov made *On The Red Front*, a film in which he deliberately employed the narrative-cutting techniques of American chase films and of *Intolerance*. By the time he returned to Moscow, the famine and the blockade were at their worst. Kuleshov found himself with a lot of enthusiastic pupils but with no possibility of getting raw film. Consequently his workshop exercised themselves by creating the subsequently famous 'films without film'. 'We prepared several instructional *études* in the form of complete little plays, arranged with "montage" changes and without pauses. . . .'

The 'films without film' were to stand the workshop in good stead when it came to experiments with actual film, around January 1923. Simple as were Kuleshov's montage experiments (which we should probably date at this time, rather than as he now does, in 1917) they formed the foundation of an entirely new phase of film art.

Kuleshov's first feature film, made with the members of his workshop, was *The Strange Adventures of Mr West in the Land of the Bolsheviks* (1924). Subsequently he went on to make *The Death Ray* (1925), *Dura Lex* (or, *By The Law*) (1926), *The Journalist Girl* (1927), *The Happy Canary* (1929), *Two-Buldi-Two* (1929), *Forty Hearts* (1931), *The Great Consoler* (1933), *The Siberians* (1940), *Happening on the Volcano* (1941), *Timour's Oath* (1943), *We From the Urals* (1944).

A teacher of remarkable gifts, Kuleshov's personal influence extended right into the 1970s. The material in this article comes from an interview recorded in Moscow on 14 July 1965.

The Origins of Montage

My now famous experiments in montage must have been round about 1917 I think. But first it is necessary to say something about the beginnings of my career.

I began to work in the cinema in 1916 when I was only seventeen years old. I was studying painting, and the producer Khanzhonkov invited me to join his studios. I was to do the décors for a film by a very celebrated director of those times, Yevgeni Bauer. Already, in Tsarist Russia there were two progressive directors: Bauer and Protazanov. I made several films with Bauer, became friendly with him and learnt a great deal from him; but unhappily he died very soon afterwards, in 1917. Then I began to design for other directors, always dreaming of directing myself. But of course, people were hesitant about entrusting me with a first film! This lack of confidence was understandable: I wanted to direct in a way which at that time was not allowed and seemed unallowable. I was the first in Russia to speak the word 'montage', to speak of the action, of the dynamic of the cinema, of realism in the art of the film. At that time all this seemed very strange indeed. They regarded me as a futurist – the name under which they lumped together all artists with Leftist tendencies. All the same, in 1917, before the October Revolution, I succeeded in directing a film which was called *The Project of Engineer Prite*. This was the first Russian film made according to the

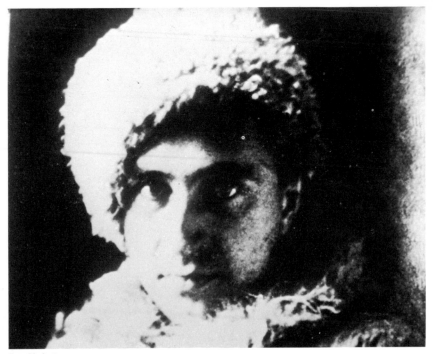

Lev Kuleshov

conception of montage, with images deliberately planned and assembled according to the laws of editing.

In making this film I took into account a whole series of peculiarities proper to cinematographic montage. Let us suppose that in a certain place we are photographing a certain object. Then, in a quite different place, we film people looking at this object. We edit the whole thing, alternating the image of the object and the image of the people who are looking at it. In *The Project of Engineer Prite*, I show people looking at electric pylons in this way. It was thus that I made an accidental discovery: thanks to montage, it is possible to create, so to speak, a new geography, a new place of action. It is possible to create in this way new relations between the objects, the nature, the people and the progress of the film. This led me to write some articles, one of which was published in *The Monitor of Cinematography*, in 1917. These articles are preserved in the archives of VGIK. My own archives are at the moment in such frightful disorder that I don't even know what remains of them: many things were lost during the war and more have been scattered by careless publishers who take them and never give them back.

These first experiments led me to devote myself specifically to montage. When I came to Paris in 1962 to present my film *The Great Consoler* at UNESCO, I was asked a very invidious question: in my opinion who first made montage in the cinema – Griffith or Kuleshov? Historically, I think it was Griffith. But the credit for the first theoretical studies on montage must perhaps go to me, despite my extreme youth at the time. In any case, though, when it is the moment for something new to make its appearance in art, the idea is already in the air. In this respect I quoted an example. I said, 'Gentlemen, have you seen a monkey catching flies? He does not catch them, he gathers them from the air, he just takes them, just like that! . . . That is the way with art: the moment arrives when you can snatch ideas from the air, because a given period of civilization and culture has put them there. Fate decreed that I should be the one. . . .'

Still in 1917 I made a film with the actor Polonsky, a star of those days: *An Unfinished Love Song*. It was a purely commercial film of no particular interest. By this time the Revolution was on its way. The private studios closed their doors.

The Revolution came. I began to work as a documentarist, as head of news films. In fact, however, I had two different activities at this time. When we had no film, I occupied myself with experiments in montage. I took old films and re-edited them in different ways. I reassembled different scenes and sequences in various ways. And it is at this time that I carried out the experiment known as the 'Kuleshov effect' – the montage of the same shot of the actor Mosjoukin in quite different contexts, producing contrasting situations.

I could not continue these experiments because I left for the front. I took part in the Civil War, and it was there that my second activity had its place: I made documentaries on the war. For cameraman I had Edward Tissé, who was later to work with Eisenstein. Tissé displayed absolute prodigies of courage in the pursuit of good shots.

One day for instance we set off in a lorry. I, as director, had charge of the machine-gun. Tissé occupied himself with the heavy and cumbrous Debrie camera. When we were about 300 metres from the Whites' guns, they opened fire on us. Tissé managed to film thirty exploding shells all of which were intended for us. When we finally abandoned the truck, the thirty-first blew it to bits. All these thirty explosions had been filmed by Tissé on a hand-cranked camera. All this is very interesting but is taking us off the point. . . . However, before leaving the subject of newsreels, I would like to recall that I was often working under the direct orders of Lenin. It was on his instructions that I went to the front, then that I made several documentaries around Moscow. With the cameraman Levitsky, who died in 1965, I filmed the first 'Subbotnik',* on 1 May 1920. This was the historic day when I first filmed Lenin. As I was always thinking about montage, to make up for the immobility of the cameras, I was all the time moving about, indicating to the cameraman where and how he was to film. It was in this way that I found myself standing beside Lenin, taking the best shots of him which exist. I was

---

* 'Subbotnik' (from 'Subbota' = Saturday): a rest-day on which workers devoted themselves to works of social importance.

busy giving instructions to the cameraman, and at times my hand is on Lenin's shoulder in order to arrange a set-up. I am glad that all these films still exist. They are preserved in the Lenin Museum.

But to get back to the 'Kuleshov effect'. At the end of 1917, by which time I was already a *Soviet* director, I tried various effects and combinations of montage. Everything that has been written on this subject is at once true and false, because the only people to whom I explained my experiments were my students. One of them was Pudovkin. Now when Pudovkin gave a lecture at the Sorbonne, the chairman of the session introduced him as the man who had created montage effect. Pudovkin corrected this immediately (he spoke French fluently), saying that the effect had been discovered by his teacher, Kuleshov. He later repeated this in his book. For my part I have related the details of the experiment in various works. The shot of Mosjoukin, always identical, was variously juxtaposed – now with a plate of soup, now with a prison gate, now with images suggesting some erotic situation. I recall that there was also a montage with a child's coffin. In short, all sorts of combinations. Unhappily no stills or notes have been preserved. The pictures that have been published abroad, as for instance in an issue of *Cinéma pratique* in 1962, are not mine at all. Mine were not kept.

I assure you that I have no complaints to make: even with the apocryphal documents, my thought and my idea have been quite correctly translated.

In any case I think that the experiments carried out subsequently in collaboration with my students were much more interesting. I was Professor at the State School of Cinema, which is today VGIK. I was teaching there from 1 May 1920. Alexandra Khoklova was already my pupil; and since then we have never been parted, but have always worked together. In 1966 we celebrated the fiftieth anniversary of our work together in the cinema. . . .

Yes; the experiments which followed those of the 'Kuleshov effect' are extremely interesting. They were concerned with 're-created space'; the action takes place in different places while the actors follow a single dramatic line, as if these quite separate places were adjacent to each other. Sadoul discusses them in detail in *Les Lettres Françaises* of 18 October 1962, and also publishes texts by Khoklova and myself. Sadoul calls his article *Mon Ami*, by which he means me. He relates my experiment in montage, transposing the action from Moscow to Paris to make the example clearer.

What I think was much more interesting was the creation of a woman who had never existed. I did this experiment with my students. I shot a scene of a woman at her toilette: she did her hair, made up, put on her stockings and shoes and dress. . . . I filmed the face, the head, the hair, the hands, the legs, the feet of different women, but I edited them as if it was all one woman, and, thanks to the montage, I succeeded in creating a woman who did not exist in reality, but only in the cinema. Hardly anyone has written about this last experiment. I kept the montage for a long time, until it was lost during the war. Everything has been lost. I never repeated this experiment or tried to repeat it. The fact is that to do it you have to be very young, as I was at the time. Then I could handle film with such boldness!

At the start two factors guided me towards montage. First the films of Griffith, and the American cinema of that period, so different from the Russian cinema of Tsarist times. The American cinema was indeed quite distinct from all other European cinemas, too: Swedish, Italian, French, with Max Linder. . . . I was always struck by the reaction of audiences to American films. The reaction was violent, and showed how much the audience was carried away by the film, the extent to which they lived the action on the screen. I thought a lot about this and arrived at the conclusion that the power of this cinema lay in the montage and in the use of close-ups, methods which were never used by the Russian film-makers. This was the first influence on me.

The second was Russian literature. Two men. And above all, Leo Tolstoy. In my book *Fundamentals of cinema mise en scène* I quote a letter in which Tolstoy speaks of montage, calling it 'connection'. He says astonishing things without knowing anything about the cinema, for the very good reason that the cinema did not exist at the time this letter was written. Yet the whole construction of Tolstoy's works is extremely 'montagist'. Pushkin, too, uses montage. You can take any poem by Pushkin, number the shots, and you have a true cinema *découpage*, ready to shoot just as it is.

All this taken together – the Americans, and Griffith in particular, Tolstoy and Pushkin – convinced me of the necessity to consider montage as the basic means of cinema art, the specific and fundamental quality of the medium. It appears to me that every art has its own specific quality, which is what makes it an art. Painting cannot exist without colours; sculpture without plastic material. The cinema consists of fragments and the assembly of those fragments, of the assembly of elements which in reality are distinct. Much later, having become adult and abandoned direction for teaching – teaching has always excited me – I discovered in Hemingway the confirmation of my idea: he, too, always wrote according to the principles of montage.

I made a lot of films. Some were failures; some were more successful; others were better still. Among these last there is one that I would particularly like to cite. It does not exist any longer: it was not preserved even though it was made under Lenin's personal directive. It was called *On The Red Front* and was made on the Western Front during the fighting with the White Poles. It was an agit-film in two reels, partly staged and partly documentary. Actual war material was mixed with staged sequences showing the daily life of the front line. Looking back, it seems very much a method of today – there is a Soviet film of 1964 called *Katiusha* which uses similar methods; indeed I think that the half-documentary, half-fiction method is one of the most interesting tendencies of contemporary cinema. I shot *On The Red Front* when I was already teaching at the School of Cinema, in 1920. My pupils Khoklova, Reich (now in Germany) and Leonid Obolensky – who often worked with me and was my assistant, and is now a television director in Tcheliabinsk – appear in it.

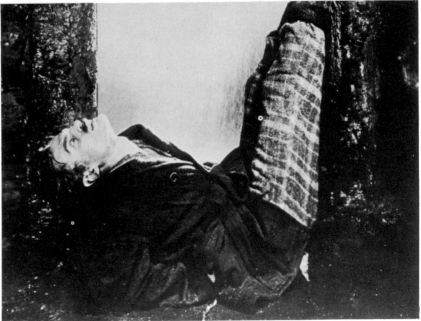

Dura Lex (Kuleshov, 1926)

Dura Lex

The Great Consoler (Kuleshov, 1933)

My next film, made with the entire team of my students, was *The Strange Adventures of Mr West in the Land of the Bolsheviks*. Then came *The Death Ray*, which was not too well thought of at home. Admittedly it was too conscious an imitation of the American cinema. There were too many tricks in it: I wanted to demonstrate all the resources of my students, all that they could do; and in consequence it is a catalogue of devices. All the same the film had a certain purely cinematographic interest.

The next film, and one of my best, was *According to the Law*, or *Dura Lex*. A great deal has been written about it. The film was entirely based on montage, and made use of a very extreme kind of acting. It contains sharp satire. After enjoying great success on its first appearance, it has become a classic of Soviet cinema.

I will mention only one more of my films, *The Great Consoler*, based on the works of the American writer O. Henry. The film is principally interesting because it is constructed on three different planes. First there is the actual life of O. Henry himself in prison; then the life of the heroine, taken from the stories of the writer. She consoles herself by reading the author's tales: in reality she is profoundly unhappy because the consoling stories cannot resolve the social problems. Finally the third dramatic line of the film is the novel by O. Henry about the safe-breaker Jimmy Valentine. He has a tragic fate: after sixteen years in prison he is promised his freedom if he will open a safe in which are locked certain important documents. He opens the safe after having smoothed his finger-ends, in order to discover the combination more easily; but in spite of the promise, he is not liberated but dies of consumption in prison. I have shown all this and I have also shown how O. Henry modified the story of Jimmy Valentine, giving it rather a rosy atmosphere, pitching it up, and giving it a happy ending – the marriage of Valentine with the banker's daughter. These three lines of action, these three different styles compose the film which I think is the most interesting of all my sound pictures. I think that it has certain elements which look forward to the things that people are doing today.*

I would like to say something about my relationship with Eisenstein, since his influence upon my work has been enormous. I regard him as the greatest of all directors and I am proud – and at the same time a little embarrassed – to say that Eisenstein was my pupil. In fact, only for a little while. Eisenstein himself used to say that anyone could be a film director, only while some would learn the job in three years, others would need three hundred years. He actually studied with me for three months. He used to come every evening. At that time we had no film. Eisenstein would come to my studio, which was known as 'Kuleshov's workshop', and every night we would spend hours doing exercises in montage – without film – particularly of mass scenes. From this arise certain points in common and similarities between, say, the mass scenes in *Strike*, and the same kind of scenes in *The Death Ray*. We had the same method and the same way of perception. Of course Eisenstein was a genius, while I am probably just possessed of a certain gift; and what I was able to discover in cinema, Eisenstein's genius developed with an extraordinary power which was able to transform it into something authentically Soviet and revolutionary. He was the first to create the revolutionary cinema. If I was able to make a revolution in cinema form, he was able to create a new and revolutionary cinema. He is alone and unique of his kind.

All that is very important to me. I am proud of it and I will never forget him. He and I always remained good friends and when I defended my doctorate thesis, he responded to my exposition. His very last letter was addressed to me.† That is why, speaking about my own work, I must acknowledge my best and my greatest friends: Eisenstein first, then Alexandra Sergeyevna Khoklova, Obolensky and Skvortsov, who is now artistic director of the Byelorusfilm Studios. As a teacher at VGIK, Skvortsov

---

* In the O. Henry story, *The Conversion of Jimmy Valentine*, the hero pays his penalty. He saves a child who is locked in the safe, thus revealing his real profession. Alexandra Khoklova who was present at this interview defined the three 'montage lines' of the film as

1. O. Henry in prison, where he meets Valentine (based on fact);
2. O. Henry's version of Jimmy Valentine's story;
3. Dulcie, the reader: the effect upon her of this story.

† An unfinished article on colour in the cinema, written in the form of a letter to Kuleshov, on which Eisenstein was working at the time of his death on 10 February 1948.

Lev Kuleshov

worked a great deal with me, among other things on *The Great Consoler*. He is a fine teacher, as was Eisenstein.

Among my students was Boris Barnet, whom I liked very much and whom I regarded as a man of very great talent. Some of his works are truly brilliant. . . . I liked Pudovkin's early films, but it seems to me that the more films he made, the less successful he became. That is a strictly personal opinion. When a man becomes too celebrated it is sometimes hard for him to carry the weight of his glory. You have to know how to be celebrated. You have to be Chaplin to know how to carry the burden of real grandeur. Not everyone can manage it. . . . But as an actor Pudovkin was quite astonishing! I prefer of all his films the early silents. His talking pictures leave me unmoved; they are not the kind of things I like. But, again, it's strictly a personal view.

I love the job of professor. At present it is not easy to recruit teachers to VGIK, because people do not want to teach, to instruct others. Directors prefer to make their own films. I on the contrary have always thought that it was more important to create men of the cinema rather than to make films myself. Eisenstein felt the same. But people like us are rather uncommon. Young people recoil in front of this task. I think that it is only a passing phase, however. Just think: eighty per cent of Soviet film-makers are old VGIK students.

And fifty per cent are my students.

(Recorded in Moscow, 14 July 1965)

5. Dziga Vertov

The aggressive, urgent and eccentric style of these fragments is expressive of the man. Dziga Vertov (born Denis Arkadievitch Kaufman on 2 January 1896) was the founder of Soviet – and one might add, world – documentary. He studied at the Psycho-Neurological Institute in Moscow, but after the October Revolution worked in the newsreel section of the new Soviet cinema. He established, directed and edited the weekly newsreel *Kinonedielia* (1918–19) and the periodical reportage *Kino-Pravda* (1922–5). He headed a group of experimental documentarists who took the name Kinoki, or Kino-Eyes. As a militant theorist he proclaimed the supremacy of what would now be called *cinéma-vérité*, life *'prise sur le fait'*. Yet as a passionate revolutionary, Dziga Vertov could not help imposing his own personality upon his material, giving his documents an extraordinarily expressive and invigorating power. He generally wrote his own scenarios. His films and his theoretical writings have had an enormous and lasting influence on world cinema – an influence which is, perhaps, only now being fully appreciated in the Anglo-Saxon cinemas.

His complete filmography is: *Kinonedielia* (43 numbers, 1918–19), *Anniversary of the Revolution* (1919), *The Mironov Trial* (1919), *Opening of the Reliquary of Sergei Radonejski* (1919), *The Battle of Tsaritsyn* (1920), *Agit-train 'Vtsik'* (1921), *History of the Civil War* (1922), *Trial of the S.R.* (1922), *Goskinocalender* (55 issues, 1923–5), *Kino-Pravda* (23 issues, 1922–5), *Yesterday, Today, Tomorrow* (1923), *Spring Pravda* (1923), *Black Sea – Icy Ocean – Moscow* (1924), *Pioneer Pravda* (1924), *Lenin Kino-Pravda* (1924), *In the Heart of the Peasants Lenin Lives* (1925), *Radio-Kino-Pravda* (1925), *Give Us Air!* (1924), *Kino-Eye* (1st series, 1924), *Forward, Soviet!* (1926), *Sixth Part of the World* (1926), *The Eleventh* (1928), *The Man with the Movie Camera* (1929), *Donbas Symphony* (1930), *Three Songs of Lenin* (1934), *Lullaby* (1937), *Memories of Serge Ordzhonikidze* (1937), *Glory to Soviet Heroines* (1938), *Three Heroines* (1938), *In the Region of Height A* (1941), *Blood for Blood, Death for Death* (1941), *News Men in the Line of Fire* (1941), *For You, Front* (1942), *In the Mountains of Ala-Tau* (1944), *The Oath of the Young* (1944), *News of the Day* (newsreel; Vertov contributed to 55 issues between 1944 and 1954). Dziga Vertov died on 12 February 1954.

(This check-list has been compiled from the filmography established by Y. Y. Vertov-Svilov for Nikolai Abramov's *Dziga Vertov*, Moscow, 1962.)

Kino-Eye: The Embattled Documentarists

How Did It Begin?
From my earliest years. By inventing fantastic tales, poems, verse satires and epigrams.

Then, in adolescence, this turned into a passion for the montage of stenograms and phonograms. Into an interest in the possibilities of transcribing documentary sound. Into experiments in transcribing in words and letters the sound of a waterfall, a saw, etc. In my 'sound laboratory' I created documentary compositions and musico-literary word-montages.

Then – in the spring of 1918 – discovery of the cinema. Began to work for the magazine *Film Week*. Meditations on the armed eye, on the role of the camera in the exploration of life. First experiments in slow-motion filming, the concept of the Kino-Eye as slow-motion vision (reading thoughts in slow motion).

. . . The Kino-Eye is conceived as 'what the eye does not see', as the microscope and the telescope of time, as telescopic camera lenses, as the X-ray eye, as 'candid camera' and so on.

These different definitions are all comprehended, for the term Kino-Eye implies:

All cinematographic means.
All cinematographic images.
All processes capable of revealing and showing truth.

(Written in 1944)

Dziga Vertov in a publicity still for *The Man with the Movie Camera* (1929)

On the Importance of Newsreel
For almost a year I have taken no part in discussions either as speaker or opposition.

We Kino-Eyes took a decision: to replace verbal discussions, which belong to literature, by cine-discussions, that is to say by creating cine-objects.

And we create them with complete success: our newsreel competes very well with the best fiction films.

The newsreel, of which *Kino-Pravda* is the most accomplished example, is boycotted by the distributors, by the bourgeois and the semi-bourgeois public. But this has not caused us to compromise and adapt it to established tastes. It has simply obliged us to change our audience.

Kino-Pravda is shown daily in numerous workers' clubs in Moscow and the provinces – with great success. And if an audience of NEP-men prefers love stories or crime stories, that does not signify that our work is not suitable. It means that the public is not suitable.

If you wish, comrades, continue with your discussions about whether the cinema is an art or not.

Continue to ignore our existence and our work.

Once again I assure you:

Kinonedielia [Film Week] No. 38 (Dziga Vertov, 1920)

The direction for the development of the revolutionary cinema has been found.
The way passes right over the heads of actors and over the roofs of the
studios, directly into life and the true multi-dramatic and multi-detective*
reality.

(1923)

From a Kino-Eye Discussion
If we want to understand clearly the effect of films on the audience, we have
first to agree about two things:

1. What audience?
2. What effect upon the audience are we talking about?

On the movie-house *habitué*, the ordinary fiction film acts like a cigar or
cigarette on a smoker. Intoxicated by the cine-nicotine, the spectator sucks
from the screen the substance which soothes his nerves. A cine-object made
with the materials of newsreel largely sobers him up, and gives him the
impression of a disagreeable-tasting antidote to the poison.

---

* At the time there was a determined effort to create a 'red detective' genre – an equivalent to
American and French police films, but with authentically Soviet characters. One example was
Dovzhenko's *The Diplomatic Bag*.

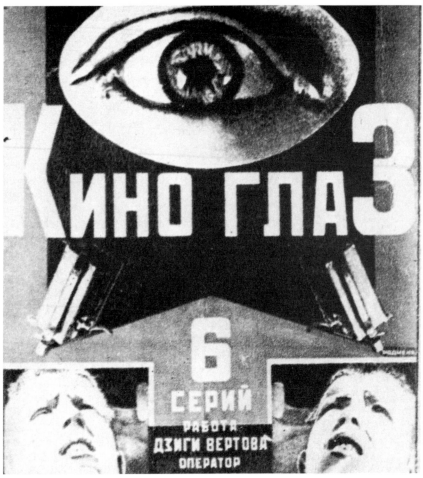

Poster by Rodchenko for *Kino-Eye*, 1924

Quite the opposite effect is produced in the case of the virgin spectator who has never seen cinema, and therefore has not been exposed to the fiction film. His education, his habit will start from the film which we shall show him. If, after a course of our *Kino-Pravda* we show him a fiction film, he will find it as bitter as a non-smoker would find his first strong cigarette.

We import quite enough of this tobacco from abroad. Amongst it, it should be said, there are a good many more fag-ends than cigarettes. The cine-cigarettes go to the best theatres, the fag-ends are destined for the provinces, the masses.

To intoxicate and suggest – the essential method of the fiction film approximates it to a religious influence, and makes it possible after a certain time to keep a man in a permanent state of over-excited unconsciousness. . . . Musical shows, theatrical and cine-theatrical performances and so on above all act upon the subconscious of the spectator or listener, distorting his protesting consciousness in every possible way.

Consciousness or Subconsciousness

We rise against the collusion between the 'director-enchanter' and the public which is submitted to the enchantment.

The conscious alone can fight against magical suggestions of every kind.

The conscious alone can form a man of firm convictions and opinions.

We need conscious people, not an unconscious mass, ready to yield to any suggestion.

Long live the consciousness of the pure who can see and hear!

Down with the scented veil of kisses, murders, doves and conjuring tricks!

Long live the class vision!

Long live Kino-Eye!

Fragments From a Journal

Our movement is called Kino-Eye. Those of us who fight for the idea of Kino-Eye call ourselves Kino-Eyes. . . . We have many enemies. This is essential. Of course it hinders our bringing our ideas into life. But on the other hand it throws us into the struggle, and sharpens our thoughts.

We are carrying the battle against art cinema, and it is hurled back at us a hundredfold. With the fragments left over by the art cinema – and often without means of any kind – we build our cine-objects.

Kino-Pravda has been kept out of the theatres, but the opinion of the public and of the independent press could not be disguised. *Kino-Pravda* has been greeted unequivocally as a turning-point in Russian cinema.

(1924)

Saw [René Clair's] *Paris Qui Dort* at the Arts Cinema. Troubled.

For two years I have had an idea to do a film exactly on these lines from the point of view of technique. I have constantly sought the opportunity to make this film. Never had the opportunity. Now – it's been done abroad.

Kino-Eye has lost one of its positions of attack. Too much delay between the thought, the conception, the plan and the realization. If we don't have the possibility of realizing our innovations at the time we invent them, we run the risk of constantly inventing and never realizing our inventions in practice.

12 April 1926

The Eleventh (extract from shooting diary)

Trumpet blast – the signal. Pause. The workers scatter. Horsemen patrol the area of the explosions. A bell. Pause. Other bells slowly answer. Tiny

The Man with the Movie Camera

figures (seen in the distance) prepare to light the fuses. Rapid ringing of bells. The men light the fuses and run for shelter. Explosion. Then another. A series of explosions, one after the other. Stones and sand gush upwards. Fragments fly, landing on rails, on cars, on cranes. Drum like rain on top of the lorry under which we are sheltering. Fly as far as the open tomb where a Scythian has lain for two thousand years. Beside the skeleton, a spear, bronze-tipped arrows with holes to contain poison. A broken pottery cup. At his head, mutton bones (for food) and the skeleton of a war-horse. The Scythian looks with hollow eyes, black openings in his skull. As if listening to the explosions. Above him – sky and clouds. Rails go right beside the tomb. On the rails run 40-ton cranes, loaded trains. Beyond the rails, the scaffold for a water-tower which is being built, equipment, lorries, and thousands of men armed with sledge-hammers and picks. The Scythian in his tomb – and the noise of new life on the move.

The Scythian in his tomb – and the cameraman Kaufman astonished, capturing on film this two-thousand-year-old silence.

Once when I was a child, my neighbour copied my essay. I got a zero (for copying) while he obtained the best mark. This neighbour was a sharp lad and enjoyed life. He did not like to think seriously and, as they say nowadays

The Man with the Movie Camera

'lived by the D system'. His life was easy and happy and he was very pleased with his homework, copied from mine.

In Germany the last part of my film *The Eleventh* was shown under a different title and signed by someone else. A year later when I came to present *The Eleventh* in Germany, I was accused of plagiarism. Only with considerable difficulty was the truth of the matter brought to light.

(1934)

In cinema, thoughts are most easily translated by montage; but I am not asked for a film-thought, but a film-case, a film-event, a film-adventure. . . .

And yet I could think on film if the chance presented itself one day. . . .

Lenin said that you must know the thing you talk about or write about.

To be able to talk about what you have not seen and do not know is a very special kind of ability, which, unhappily, a lot of people have. I haven't this facility, as it happens.

I succeeded, by and large, in making *Three Songs of Lenin* accessible, comprehensible to millions of spectators. But it was not done at the price of giving up a cinematographic language. Not at the cost of rejecting processes found in the past.

What matters above all is the unity of form and of content. It is not permis-

Three Songs of Lenin (Dziga Vertov, 1934)

Filming for *Kino-Pravda* (*c.* 1924)

sible to trouble the audience with some trick or process which does not come naturally out of the content and which is not demanded by circumstances.

In 1933, thinking about Lenin, I decided to turn to the springs of popular art. As events proved . . . I was right to do so.

I would like to continue on this route.

The acquaintance with authentic documents of popular art had a great influence on me. Firstly, these songs were song-documents. As is well known, the documentary arm has always interested me most of all. Secondly, beneath their apparent simplicity, the songs are powerful, vivid, remarkably sincere. Finally their main characteristic: unity of *form and content*; in other words precisely that quality which we writers, composers, film-makers have not achieved up to the present.

(February 1936)

The New Babylon (Kozintsev and Trauberg, 1929)

6. Grigori Mikhailovitch Kozintsev

Kozintsev's lively reminiscences of life in Kiev and Petrograd during and immediately after the civil war, and of a youngster's thrilling discovery of art and the artistic gods of those times – above all Mayakovski and Meyerhold – admirably complement the memories of Yutkevitch, his senior by barely a year, and a comrade in the Factory of the Eccentric Actor. Like Yutkevitch, Kozintsev has never lost the air of youthfulness and curiosity of those FEKS days; and his *Hamlet* (1964) and *King Lear* (1970) show how completely he has retained his creative gift for more than four decades.

Born on 22 March 1905, Kozintsev studied painting at the Academy of Fine Arts in Petrograd. In 1921 he organized FEKS, in company with Yutkevitch and the writer and director Leonid Trauberg (born 1902). Their theatre had as its prime aim the search for new forms of theatrical art – and subsequently cinema. From the 'eccentricity' of *The Adventures of Oktyabrina*, the expressionism of *The Overcoat* and the romanticism of *S.V.D.*, FEKS arrived at the realism of *Alone*. The triumph of the group came, however, with Kozintsev and Trauberg's trilogy about the fictional hero, *Maxim*, who was subsequently to pass into Soviet folklore. Yutkevitch having early left the group, Kozintsev and Trauberg continued to work together until 1947. Since then Trauberg has worked mostly as a scenarist, while Kozintsev's best work has been his remarkable series of adaptations from literary classics – *Don Quixote, Hamlet* and *King Lear*. Since 1922 Kozintsev has devoted much time to teaching and writing.

Films in collaboration with Trauberg: *The Adventures of Oktyabrina* (1925), *Mishka against Yudenitch* (1925), *The Devil's Wheel* (1926), *The Overcoat* (1926), *Little Brother* (1927), *S.V.D.* (1927), *New Babylon* (1929), *Alone* (1931), *The Youth of Maxim* (1934), *Return of Maxim* (1937), *The Vyborg Side* (1938), *Film-Notes on Battles No. 1 and 2* (1941; with Lev Arnshtam), *Simple People* (1945; released in 1956).

Films by Kozintsev alone: *Pirogov* (1947), *Belinsky* (1951), *Don Quixote* (1957), *Hamlet* (1964), *King Lear* (1970).

The following article has been compiled from extracts from Kozintsev's book *The Deep Screen* and interviews conducted in Moscow in July 1965.

A Child of the Revolution

I was born in Kiev and attended the gymnasium there. It was a queer kind of education we had in the first years of the Revolution. Classes were frequently interrupted by artillery fire, and when I left school in the evening, with my satchel stuffed with books, you could never be sure who was currently occupying the town. The Austro-Hungarian occupiers had been replaced by Petliura's men. At Petchersk, not far from the gymnasium, the twisted corpses of shot men lay in the ditch. Our teachers described the flora and fauna of Africa, explained the conjugation of Latin verbs; and meanwhile machine-guns chattered in the suburbs. In the night you heard the hooves of cavalry detachments trotting by; or the inky southern silence would be rent by shots; or by a cacophony of cries, bangs, gratings: thundering, drumming, echoing, howling. It was bandits trying to break down the gates of the house, and the guard-pickets formed by the tenants shaking sheets of tin, hammering on stoves and brass plates, calling for help from goodness knows whom. Came the dawn. And again, satchel in hand, I would trot by broken windows, walls scarred with bullets, encountering armed men absurdly decked out in blue frock-coats.* Death stalked the town. People spoke of death with no respect: 'They've stuck him to the wall,' 'he's done with profit and loss,' 'they've made small change of him,' 'they've done for him.' Distantly the artillery

---

* The uniform of Petliura's nationalists.

rumbled. The urchins would stop, listen, discuss the calibre of the guns. People had learned to distinguish the different sounds of the different types. In Vassilievsky Street, the crowd escorted a black-marketeer who had speculated in foodstuffs in short supply. They dragged him, hung about with the rotten herrings which he had sold. Men forced a way through the crowd to hit him violently. The blood, which seemed remarkably red, stained the face of the speculator, pouring on to his shirt and on the herrings, making him monstrous. My memory retained these images: they came in useful for *The Vyborg Side*. I saw with my own eyes Shchors' troops enter the town, and the detachments of the First Cavalry Army. This was in 1919.

On the walls of buildings were proclamations: 'What does the red star signify?' Men wearing the red star on their caps and their fur hats liberated Kiev. These men had chased out the occupiers and the bandits; they stopped the pogroms and the summary executions; they established the People's Government. And immediately, in the revolutionary town, every kind of art began to flourish. Men full of go and jollity took over the tables and the chairs of the officers of the Ukrainian Department of Arts. Innumerable committees, sections and subsections discussed projects for producing all the great classic plays of the world, for organizing popular festivals and for decorating the squares in honour of the first of May. Theatre studios and art studios proliferated. Everyone took to art with passion, and with passion people taught it. What was not taught? There were lectures on the troubadours and minstrels, on the Baroque art of the Ukraine, and on the Japanese theatre. The Diaghilev dancer Bronislava Nijinska directed Stravinski's *Petrushka*. The future academician M. P. Alexeiev created a theatrical repertory.

I did not only study at the gymnasium. In the evenings I went to the school of painting, to the classes given to a little group of young people by Alexandra Exter. A still-life composition had been set before us: apples on a napkin, a pot of sand. We had to represent these objects, but other images obsessed my mind: I heard the brass of a military band; the characters of well-loved books came and went before my eyes, violently, strangely lit as if by footlights; sparks flew from clashing swords; I saw the gleaming green eyes of the wizard from Gogol's *The Frightful Vengeance*, and, spurring their horses, the Three Musketeers, leaping ravines. In fact I did not do at all well with still-lifes; but I invented parodies, I drew caricatures, I designed décors for imaginary plays. Some of my older comrades in the studio, S. Vishnevskaia, I. Rabinovitch, A Tichler and N. Chifrin, already accomplished painters, were entrusted with the job of decorating a propaganda train. They adopted me into their team, although I knew how to do nothing. They were friendly towards me, I suppose, because of my youth and enthusiasm, and they even allowed me to decorate one of the wagons on my own. We joined the train on the far bank of the Dnieper, where it was being prepared. No sooner had we arrived than I tried for the first time to mount an agit-sketch, a short propaganda play. It was performed in a goods wagon, with the open doors providing the stage. The soldiers (our audience) sat on the ground in front.

That was real happiness! After the narrow formulas of school, these words which spoke of the majesty of labour, of social justice, of the final and decisive struggle seemed to come from some marvellous story-book. And the thing that was most amazing in this new life was that I, a mere lad, could take part in it, work for it. Later, and there I am in an army cart on the way to Kiev after the departure of the train for the front. On my knees, my military ration, my worker's bread. Later still and I am taking part in decorating the town, in company with the same painters. At night in a lorry loaded with painted plywood (we were to fix the panels on the house-fronts), lying on the rocking heap of wooden posters, we yelled as we drove through the dark and empty streets the verses that had just reached us from Petrograd:

Enough tuppenny truths!
Sweep the rubbish out of your heads!
The streets are our paint-brushes,
The squares are our palettes!...*

To sweep the old rubbish out of my head was not particularly difficult: I still knew very few truths, even tuppenny ones.

And then there opened up before me the gates of a universe which I scarcely dared dream about. The painter Isaac Rabinovitch, engaged by the former Solvtzovsky Theatre (now the Lenin Theatre), knew my passion and took me with him as an assistant. My work was not very complicated: I had to dilute the gum colours in stoneware pots, soak an enormous brush in the colour selected by the painter, and daub it on the drop, spread out on the floor of the scenery shop.

After a rehearsal one day I took my courage in both hands and handed my sketches to the director, Mardjanov. He looked at them carefully and said that he was going to put me in touch with another young painter and that together we might do the décors for one of his new productions. Immediately there appeared in front of me a boy of my own age, with a pointed nose, lively eyes, dressed in a well-ironed shirt with many pleats, and green trousers. On his head he wore a check cap, and he was twirling a little cane between his fingers. He was called Seriozha; and his surname was Yutkevitch.

Mardjanov asked us to do the décors for the operetta *La Mascotte*. And what was marvellous – he talked to us as if he had forgotten our youth! The famous master, who had worked with great painters, talked to two lads as if they were distinguished designers. He gave us the text of the play, annotated by himself, explained his ideas and the scenic possibilities. Konstantin Alexandrovich seemed to find this commission perfectly natural and seemed to have no doubts about our abilities. It is difficult for me to know now whether this was just his way of encouraging us, whether he really had confidence in our youthful abilities, or whether he was simply seduced by our enthusiasm. Anyway, we started to make sketches for the décors. But already

---

* 'Order to the Army of Art', by Mayakovski.

we had something else in our minds – the fantastic idea of organizing our own theatre was born in us and began to grow. Young actors, including Alexei Kapler the future scenarist, came to join us. We had no trouble in finding collaborators! In art, we all worshipped the same god, Mayakovski; and this common faith seemed to us decisive. By hearsay we knew his powerful bass voice, his large stature. The lucky ones possessed little books, bizarrely laid out, of his early verses – the new poems only reached us in manuscript copies. We at once learned them by heart, read them aloud and recited them in (for us) subdued voices all the day long, from morning to night. We did not clearly perceive the deeper sense of them, but the force of the rhythms and the images, the eruptive power of every line, swelled our hearts. Pleasure and joy caught our breaths: the vision of a new and marvellous world filled us with ecstasy.

Again Mardjanov listened to our projects with complete seriousness. And we left the office of the *régisseur-général* of all the theatres of Kiev armed with a paper covered with signatures and rubber stamps, which certified that a cellar formerly occupied by the cabaret 'Jimmy-le-Borgne' was placed at our disposal to be used as a theatre.

We went down a dark stairway. Striking a match, we found the keyhole. The key turned. The door opened. The room was cluttered with tables and overturned chairs. Empty bottles and bits of paper were scattered everywhere. On the little stage, the scenery hung in tatters. Silently, not daring to breathe, we went up on the stage, found the switchboard and threw the main switch. The footlights came on. True, not all the bulbs were working, but the footlights came on, real footlights. To the left, in the wings, there were ropes. We tried pulling one of them: the drop-curtain started to come down, a real drop-curtain. We raised it and lowered it several times. Then we went down into the auditorium and stacked the tables and chairs in a corner. Having unearthed a broom we carefully swept the floor, then set out the chairs in rows. Then we sat down in the front row, and stayed there a long time, silently looking at the stage. Yes, it was now *our* theatre.

For our first production we chose Mayakovski's tragedy *Vladimir Mayakovski*. Of course the deep sense of this play remained an indecipherable mystery to us, and from the first rehearsals we were clearly in a mess with it. Mardjanov listened to the story of our vexations with imperturbable gravity. He said that the play was very difficult. He did not add, 'for *you*.' No, difficult for everybody. And he advised us to devise sōmething ourselves, some kind of clownery, he said. This suggestion instantly raised up a host of ideas appropriate to our age. We all adored the circus. At that time there were some gifted clowns, Fernandez and Frico, at the Kisso Circus. They performed some classical clowning which ended in a funeral: the 'corpse' fell out of the coffin and ran after the procession with anguished cries and torrents of tears. Frico hobbled in boots three feet long and peeled off innumerable waistcoats. Fernandez sparkled with flowers and butterflies spangled on his white clown get-up. They played tunes on bottles and motor-horns, swapped blows and fled from the ring, slipping, tumbling, and producing hidden crackers from their pantaloons. It was the old popular comedy in all its poetry. There was a fantasy about the chalky face of the one and the exaggerated make-up of the other. Badly done this nonsense might seem flat and vulgar, but in the hands of true clowns, it came to life, with all the charm of its humour and irreality. Under the influence of the clowns, I wrote a circus *divertissement*. Fernandez and Frico lent us their costumes, free of charge. They attended our rehearsals and gave us practical professional advice.

But already we were caught up in other projects. Our old friend Petrushka, the puppet, rose up from behind screens abloom with painted roses, and drew us into his enchanted kingdom. We made puppets and mounted Pushkin's story *The Priest and his Servant Balda*. We began to tour the streets and the clubs. We even had the opportunity to hear applause for the first time. On the wall of my room in Leningrad still hangs one of the artists of our puppet theatre, with his bearded head drooping forward and his arms hanging by his side. Once upon a time he wagged like a fury on the stage, declaiming:

I'm the gypsy singer,
The finest of the bunch!
  I sing bass
  And I drink kvass
And pineapples I munch. . . .

The moths have eaten his velvet frock-coat, his red silk shirt has lost its colour, his gold lace is frayed. A long time has gone by since he passed into my hands from those of a barrel-organ player. I owe him a lot. He is one of those friends of my childhood with whom I was able to travel in the happy country of popular fantasy where everyone who dreams of art must tarry: Petrushka, the little clay animals from the Ukraine – sweet monsters with green or brown mouths and roaring manes – or the *images d'Epinal*, among which was a procession of mice following the funeral procession of a cat laid on a sledge. . . .

Yutkevitch's parents had left the Ukraine, and Seriozha had to go with them. Looking for a play for a new production, I came across *Tsar Maximilian*, which is a kind of popular tragedy, but with burlesque elements. I was attracted by its crude pathos and poetry. We adapted it to 'reflect actuality'. We decided to play it on a public square. Already this was a real production, with scenery, costumes (real bric-à-brac!) and even a poster. The leading role was taken by Alexei Kapler. I missed the première, because I'd caught typhoid.

Discovery of Petrograd

The notion of the avant-garde is too general. In every country it manifested itself in its own characteristic way. If you talk about FEKS, you have to remember that I was fourteen when I began my first work, and that this was in the first days of the Revolution. And the dominant influence was

Grigori Kozintsev

Mayakovski. Beyond that of course we were in touch with certain experiments in the West. In particular we knew Matisse, Picasso and Cézanne very well through the reproductions in the art books of Morozov, and the Shchukin collections of painting in Moscow. . . . Yes, we knew modern French art very well.

The Union of Art Workers of Kiev sent me to Petrograd in order to continue my studies there. The journey was made by any available means, from cattle-trucks to wagons in which one had to sit on top of heaps of scrap metal. This was during the Civil War. My only baggage was a pillow-case containing a shirt, a book of Mayakovski poems, and a series of reproductions of Picasso paintings. Truly, that was all I had with me. Petrograd astonished me by its size and its emptiness. The palaces, the avenues, the huge buildings, all seemed uninhabited and uninhabitable after the intimate lanes of Kiev, lined with chestnut trees. All this had been abandoned by people, who had left only memories behind. Through this square, Yevgeni fled, pursued by the bronze horseman; Akakii Akakievitch clip-clopped home through this lane; it was in this house that Raskolnikov became a murderer. In the icy mists, memories and monuments materialized. The Tsars, grandly mounted, crossed the dead town. Peter I unhurriedly left the Palace of Engineers; Nicholas I spurred his charger through the houses; Alexander III dozed upon his mare near where the station now lay destroyed.

People passed by. Some dragged their monthly food ration on a sledge. They had no time for traditions and remembrances. At full pelt, with a deafening noise of rattling metal, a tram wobbling all over the place would cross a square; the tramways were not running, but from time to time a solitary car would appear, its windows blinded with plywood, rushing heaven knew where, without anyone knowing either its stops or its ultimate destination. From the edge of the Moika, I turned into the Field of Mars. The un-blacked-out windows of the house on the corner attracted me. Through the dirty windows and the net of ice could be seen the mural decoration inside. Strange personages, peculiar birds and flowers could be made out under the soot-stains and damp marks. This place was the building of 'The Actor's Rest', decorated by the painter Sudekin. Here the poets and the painters of St Petersburg used to meet; here Meyerhold presented *The Scarf of Columbine*; as to that spectre in a powdered wig and tricorne hat, there in a niche, it was Count Carlo Gozzi, the Venetian story-teller who revived the Italian Comedy in the eighteenth century. I recalled again the thin booklets with covers illustrated by Golovin: in blue and yellow settings, an actor flanked by three enormous oranges, and underneath, in antique calligraphy, *The Love of Three Oranges*. We were still in Kiev when we got hold of these little booklets from somewhere and struggled vainly to understand what was printed in them. There was *Doctor Dappertutto's Diary*; that was how Vsevolod Meyerhold signed himself at that time. Doctor Dappertutto. The comedy of masks. 'The Actor's Rest'. Now it was a filthy cellar, icy, deserted. . . . Skirting heaps of snow and blocks of ice, I crossed the Field of Mars. A dead horse lay covered in snow. A patrol passed by. A gun thundered out. I stopped, thoughtful: 'Here we go! . . .'

'Where's the shooting?' I asked someone a question which would have been so normal in Kiev.

'Nowhere', came the reply. 'It's midday. Check your watch, comrade'. Thus I learnt the first of the customs of this new town.

The day after my arrival in Petrograd, I was intrigued by a great crowd massed in front of the window of a shop at the corner of 25 October Prospect. The passers-by clustered around the cracked window and read the manuscript bulletins of the Rosta Agency.* Alongside were placarded the collage posters of V. Lebedev. I was immediately struck by the joyful energy with which the art of the painter abounded. The drawing was reduced to an absolutely geometric simplicity, without sacrificing the concrete character of the figurative representation. It was the amusing simplicity of children's drawings, the vivid truth of essential features. The proletariat swept away with a single blow all the enemies of the working class; tiny bourgeois and profiteers fell under the assault of an enormous red broom, in a frenzy of little grey and yellow legs. On the neighbouring poster there advanced victorious, guns pointed menacingly, a sailor with his blue collar blowing in the wind, and a Red soldier with a yellow cloak.

Everything towards which I was unconsciously yearning was there: the power and the energy of popular imagery, the force of expression, the sheer joy of living. At the time I was probably incapable of expressing all that. But the sight of those posters put joy into my heart.

I found Mardjanov at the Palace Theatre, with its cracked marble facings and its foyer decorated with an artificial grotto. Mardjanov was director of the Comic Opera, and he at once gave orders that I was to join the Studio in the capacity of director. Then I had to find the Academy of Fine Arts and present my recommendation all covered with signatures and stamps, and to seek enrolment in the painting section. This was quite simply done. The only things that really went with the pompous title of 'Academy' were the fantastic sphinxes that reared up against the background of the frozen Neva, and the great icy hallway of the principal building. Once past these there were only little cubicles with plywood partitions and little iron stoves whose chimneys made arabesques under the ceilings. A welcoming man in a fur cap and cape admitted me into Altmann's studio. The studio was in the yard and seemed especially icy. There were not many students, but it was the same kind of joyful brotherhood as had decorated the streets of Kiev. No one bothered about cold or hunger. Life seemed marvellously interesting, and there was no doubt at all that this moment marked the coming of a new era, the era of art. This art had to be as bold as the workers' power itself, as pitiless towards the past as the Revolution. Everyone argued fiercely about 'contemporary rhythms' and 'industrial poetry' whilst chopping wood and lighting the

* Rosta: Telegraphic agency, now Tass. Its 'satire windows', with illustrations by the painter Lebedev to texts by Mayakovski, were justly famous.

stove. When that was done, smoke was added to the cold. Altmann arrives, muffled in a scarf. We seize our brushes in our frozen fingers. . . . The cannon thunders. I look calmly at my watch and set the hands to twelve o'clock. Now I'm a Petrogradite.

At this time I got to know a young man just arrived from Odessa: Leonid Trauberg. He had written a verse play, wanted to work in the theatre, and, while waiting, was working for an organization called Uprodpitokr. I never knew what this name signified. The life of art simmered around us. The extent to which we were crazed about art in those difficult years now seems quite astonishing. Exhibitions would open in half-ruined rooms; in public debates passions ran high. Poets of different (and numberless) tendencies read their verses; new names appeared constantly, and people whose names already seemed legendary continued to write. It was hard to realize that these great ones lived in the same city as I did, collected their rations, caught colds, had to get their shoes mended. In the metallic hall of the House of the People, I saw Alexander Blok leaning on the narrow balustrade of the balcony. Turning my back on the stage, not daring to breathe, I looked at his face and felt that there could be no eyes as beautiful or as sad in the whole world. Certainly it was not just the physical aspect of the poet which I was seeing in this way; for me his poetry was reflected in his appearance, making it peculiarly significant. He remained there, in his beaver hat, astonishingly impassive; and all around him sailors and their mates roared with laughter at the capers of the circus folk, men in military cloaks cried out, fellows with wild hair under fur caps chewed sunflower seeds and urchins selling cigarettes practically fell off the balcony in their delight.

In the House of Arts, on the Moika, Mayakovski's fine bass voice thundered out, and we applauded so enthusiastically that our hands swelled and reddened. People arriving from Moscow told of the October Revolution of the Theatre; and the name of Meyerhold was quoted a great deal in a flurry of rumour and argument. Previously the image of Meyerhold was linked for me with two portraits. In N. P. Ulianov's drawing, the *metteur en scène* was pictured in a white pierrot smock, with his face raised towards heaven expressing a pensive and melancholy pride. In contrast, Boris Grigoriev's painting showed an imperious person in a dress suit, with white gloves, standing like a conjurer, right foot in position for some dance step; in front, a redskin warrior bends his bow, ready to fire his arrow into the air. What, then, was this man with the face of a wise and hairy bird? Prestidigitator, hypnotist, actor in some unknown role? I thought of the description of *Balaganchik*: Clown losing all his currant-juice blood in the effervescent phantasmagoria by Blok, 'mystics' hiding their faces in painted cardboard bodies . . . symbols, bas-reliefs, cubes, masks and many other things besides, totally unintelligible for us. All this now disappeared as a vision fades.

In a military tunic, with a soldier's cloak slung over his shoulders and a revolver in his belt, back from the Southern Front comes the honorary soldier of the Red Army, the communist Meyerhold. He has torn from the stage all the Baroque which he used so much to love. Against the background of the brick wall of the building itself are nailed structures in raw wood. On the boards of the first theatre of the Russian Republic, instead of heroes in finery, there are instructors in 'Biomechanics', in workers' overalls. Smoke and the smell of powder, neighing horses, naturalism in every element. . . . At the foot of the poster, a note: 'It is permitted to enter, to exit, to whistle or to applaud during the performance.' The curtain, psychology, footlights, symbols, make-up and dramaturgy are abolished. 'Talk of "beauty" to the students of the Workers' Faculties, and they will start to whistle as if you had insulted them', Larissa Reisner wrote at this time; 'and if you mention the words "creation" or "sentiment" they will smash up the seats and leave the hall.' 'Springtime!' says a character in *Mystère-Bouffe*; 'Passer-by! Stop and wonder! Curtain!' Now you could only wonder – there was no longer any curtain. Young hotheads enthusiastically greeted every word of the new order. All were ready, at once and with no reckoning the cost, to carry out the 'Order to the Army of Art' given by Mayakovski:

Drag the pianos into the street
Wrest drums from the windows,
Prance if you like or kick if you like,
But I want the racket of tempests!

For technical reasons things did not get round to the musical instruments. It was a matter of putting into practice the two last lines. It was simpler.

Trauberg and I spent all our free time together. Coming home from the Comic Opera through dark and icy streets, squatting in front of the stove to warm up the millet (which was pretty well the staple diet of townsfolk at the time) we conceived chimeric projects. Georgii Kryjitzki, a professional *metteur en scène* – he was a grown-up – had struck up a friendship with us. Soon Yutkevitch and Kapler arrived, and a new group was born. Exploding with energy, captivated by the art of the circus and the Rosta windows, we aspired to spectacles never seen before. My modest experiments were oddly muddled in my head: street decorations, the fairground spectacle of *Tsar Maximilian*, clowning, the multi-coloured coach of a propaganda train. . . . To all this was added a whole terminology that was then very fashionable among young painters. None of us really understood it, but it seemed ultramodern; and we used it with abandon. Already in Kiev, walking through the quiet provincial roads where a carriage only rarely rattled by, we had talked about the 'pathos of urbanism', and sung the praises of the music-hall when we had never seen any performances other than classical matinées at the Solvtzovsky Theatre. In Petrograd we had seen some good eccentrics in the circus, and in the cinema the first Chaplin films. The word 'Eccentricism' seemed to us peculiarly expressive.

We organized FEKS (the Factory of the Eccentric Actor). I was then sixteen. Although we had absolutely no material means, we decided to mount a production. Serge, the talented circus performer, together with a few cabaret artists and some amateurs who had come from somewhere or other, threw themselves into our projects. Our first production, Gogol's *Marriage*, was extremely bizarre, for our own period was violently reflected in it. The play ended with Gogol himself dying in despair upon the stage. It was a case of trying to demolish all the usual theatrical forms and to find others, which could convey the intense sentiment of the new life. Unless this last point is recognized, our creations of that period would become incomprehensible. All these experiments, all these quests for new forms came because we had an intense feeling of an extraordinary renewal of life. We felt profoundly the impossibility of translating this sensation of the marvel and the importance of events through the means offered by the art of the past, which to our eyes appeared dreadfully academic and naturalist. Thus, in our production of *Marriage*, a preponderant place was accorded to rhythm, because the novelty of things was initially felt not in themes nor in characters, but in rhythm. *Art had changed rhythm.* The new epoch had found its first expression in rhythm. This was extremely interesting, because there was a sort of contradiction in it; and that is why all comparisons made between the avant-garde movements of the West and ours, seem to me to be false, and not merely in respect of the conditions of our life. What we were doing then we were doing in the cold and the famine of a devastated country. The conditions of life were very hard. The State, occupied with a full-scale Civil War, was undergoing enormous difficulties. Yet the dominant sentiment was the affirmation of life. The young artists felt life in all its richness and colour, and artistic forms seemed naturally to take on the artistic forms of a great popular carnival. In the middle of every kind of privation a sort of fair was going on. The young artists bore the common fate gaily, so fine did the time in which they lived appear to them. If this atmosphere is forgotten or neglected, then the art of those times remains incomprehensible.

So we tried to mount *Marriage*. I say 'tried' because the thing had no relation either to Gogol's play or to what one normally understands by *mise en scène*. The structure of the spectacle, an amalgam of circus, cabaret and cinema, was improvised and immediately modified as having already become old hat. We were haunted by all sorts of vague notions which were immediately supplanted by others, still more fantastic, still more imprecise. We wanted to show everything: people blown up like posters, cascades of gags, a combination of film projection and real-life actors playing in front of the screen. We gathered bits and pieces without ever thinking what the whole effect would be. I think it was the first time that anyone had used this mixture of film and living actors.* We had extracted some bits of a Chaplin film – I do not remember which; the copy was incomplete. While the film was projected on the screen, in front, in the foreground, the actors played. Some characters were dressed in the 'constructivist' style – no doubt under the influence of reproductions of Picasso's designs for the costumes for *Parade*.

* See the Eisenstein article *My First Film* (page 48). *Marriage* preceded Eisenstein's *Enough Simplicity* by six months, but came after *Iron Heel*. The mixture of actors and film had in fact been used on the stage as early as 1896, in the Châtelet production of *La Biche aux Bois*.

(As I think about it, it seems very strange that at the start of my creative work I should set out to demolish the classics, since Gogol is my favourite author; and that I should have only scorn for traditional art since my two most recent films have been adaptations from Shakespeare.) Gerassimov, who started off as an actor in our group, remembers how he came to my home for the first time. We were both of us eighteen, but I was his master and he my pupil. Such were our relationships at that time! As a first exercise I set him a transposition of *Hamlet* into pantomime and modern costume. In fact I am very glad that I went through these experiments at the age of eighteen; they have been very useful to me. Done later in life, they would have been less spontaneous, less natural. Anyway, I love to recall those years. . . . But to return to *Marriage*. . . .

We were only allowed to get on to the stage on the day of the première, and for only two hours before curtain rise. We were still rehearsing with the actors while the audience was kicking up a great din in the foyer, demanding that the doors be opened and the show begin. During this time, straddled across the proscenium barrier, a young man with a huge forehead and a lot of hair was hurrying us, dominating the other noise. 'Too slow!' he was shouting in a sharp voice; and again, 'Much too slow! Speed up the action!' It was Sergei Eisenstein. I must add one remark: we might be accused of all sorts of faults, but slowness was not one of them! However, even this helter-skelter of ours seemed too slow for Eisenstein. The public which filled the theatre was mostly youngsters, like ourselves, from innumerable workshops and studios. The audience had brought big balloons with them: during the play these balloons floated on to the stage and the actors sent them back into the auditorium. . . .

Parisiana and Sevzapkino

For the first time Yutkevitch and myself were invited to take part in an exhibition. After having hung our sketches, we placarded above them slogans in support of the 'street arts' – posters, advertisements, fairground shows. Having read these, a very learned critic dismissed us with indignation: 'If you carry on like this, you will end up saying that the cinema is an art as well.' That bothered us a lot. . . .

Our group broke up. Kapler returned to the Ukraine, Yutkevitch became designer with Foregger's Theatre in Moscow. Kryjitzki had gone off earlier after having settled up with us with some very stern criticism. As to Trauberg and myself, we actually did go from bad to worse till we ended up in cinema. Ultimately it became clear that all our tendencies and our instincts drew us to this art. We did not know where to turn for advice. A film assistant, very knowing, shook his head and said: 'Not a hope.' Still, we wrote a scenario. At the studios, we could not get past the waiting-room. After having weighed up the not very impressive appearance of the authors, they told us 'We don't need scenarios.' 'So what do you need?' we asked. 'Go to the "Parisiana" on 25 October Prospect. Over the Parisiana is Sevzapkino.* They study scenarios there.' Today the address seems symbolic. Then even words mingled capriciously.

The Franco-Russian signboard arrested the customer like a fairground advertisement: a man in a dress suit and a lady with her hand in his, against some sumptuous background, seemed to leap out of the poster. The word 'Sevzapkino' irrupted in this elegance rather like some basement tenant taking possession of a great mansion. Passing posters for *Bianca the Adventuress* and *Satan Triumphant* and photographs of a kiss-curled Harry Piel, we climbed the stairs to the fourth floor. In a meanly furnished room, the secretary, a young man with long hair and a leather jacket, was laying out on a table 'art' postcards: there were reproductions of antique statues, portraits by Repin, and photographs of ancient coaches in the Stable Museum. This young man welcomed us in a friendly way: within minutes we were on familiar terms of address, at the end of half an hour we were friends. He was a student in the Institute of Screen Art and the picture postcards were destined for the 'red corner'. This 'red corner' was not a case simply of a 'cultural measure', as we say nowadays, but of a combat action in prelude to the main assault. This young man began his studies after having worked for the Cheka (anti-smuggling section). The first thing he heard at the Institute was the word 'Gentlemen', a mode of address which appeared to be current there. The angry student rushed to the Smolny: two more young komsomols were dispatched to the cinema front. With them the student organized the 'Communist Assembly': there were three of them. Their 'red corner' was only the beginning. Friedrich Ermler (such was the young man's name) did much to implant the term 'Comrade' in the cinema. Meantime he hoped to find success as an actor. He had been promised a role in the short, *Tea*. According to Ermler's own account, the role perfectly suited his artistic personality: it required long hair and a leather jacket. He had already some experience – as an adolescent in Rejitsa in Latvia, the apprentice-chemist Ermler had gone to the local photographer in a free moment. Dressed in a hired frock-coat, with a chrysanthemum in his button-hole, he had had himself photographed in the style of the hero of a film which he had seen the day before.

The future film directors of Lenfilm Studios were already assembled in the city where they were later to make *Chapayev, The Great Citizen, Baltic Deputy*. They were still ignorant of their vocation, and did not know their future friends. Among the extras in the film *Palace and Fortress* was Sergei Vassiliev, disguised in a beard and moustache. He would not make his first film until five years later. In the magazine *Worker and Theatre*, Josif Heifetz tries his hand at journalism. Not only does he never think of cinema direction, but he does not know that this same year a student with an enthusiasm for amateur theatre is finishing technical school – Alexander Zarkhi. An adolescent, just arrived from Sverdlovsk, wanders the streets, stops in front of a hoarding,

* The word 'Sevzapkino', signifying 'North-Western Cinema' is typical of the curious abbreviated word-combinations coined in the revolutionary period.

reads the conditions for admission to the art and theatre workshops. Art tempts him, but he does not know which route to choose: soon Sergei Gerassimov will notice the poster for FEKS and come and join us. In Moscow a new film actor (or 'living model' as they used to say) is busy working in *The Adventures of Mr West in the Land of the Bolsheviks*: Vsevolod Pudovkin. At Proletkult they are rehearsing Eisenstein's production of *Gas Masks*. In a Kharkhov newspaper a young cartoonist has just made his appearance: Alexander Dovzhenko. I have before me the programme for the Petrograd cinemas during these very months: not a single Soviet film on the screens. . . .

Dishevelled and triumphant, Ermler bursts in: our scenario is accepted. An event practically incredible at that time. One of the Sevzapkino directors had said 'Rubbish.' The second was angry: 'That, eccentricism? I've just come from the USA: *that*'s what I call eccentricism!' The third, B. V. Tchaikowski, announced unexpectedly that this comedy appealed to him. The chairman of the Scientific and Artistic Committee upheld him energetically: we needed new scenarios, new styles, new strength. It was decided to make the film. Tchaikowsky was appointed artistic director of the production, and we became his assistants.

In 1924, Sevzapkino possesses one small studio, which was formerly an orangery or perhaps a photographic studio. The walls are glass, the lights, in metal troughs, from time to time fling bits of burning carbon on to the actors. The studio employs three directors and two cameramen, all specialists with a long experience of the cinema before the Revolution. Technical equipment: two ancient Pathé cameras. All bought cheap, and rather weary. When there are visitors interested in the cinema, they are above all shown the costume shop. The studio director, who serves as guide, never neglects to show a great pair of breeches made of skin: it is not any ordinary piece of clothing, but a historical pair of breeches, since Alexander III used to wear them for riding. The costumes are kept in impeccable order. In interminable ranks are hung officers' cloaks with silver fur collars, Guards uniforms, hussars' jackets, dolmans; the epaulettes gleam, the gold-lace flares, the buttons, braids and pipings dance, the plumes on the bicorns bloom, the lancers' manes cascade from gleaming shakos, the twin-headed eagles cling to the caps of the light cavalry; lying on velvet, in showcases, glitter stars, crosses, rosettes, decorations and medals.

Here, in the silence and the moth-balls, was preserved the very essence of the films they were then making. Experienced dressers put the actors into these uniforms, the make-up man had a stock of beards and moustaches sufficient for the entire House of the Romanoffs, the Palace was rebuilt inside the studio, and all these sumptuosities were drawn up in front of the cameras and the lights. The man whose beard and moustache resembled the Tsar's ordered (by means of a subtitle as long as it was eloquent) that revolutionaries should rot in prison. The aides-de-camp clicked to attention and the whole waxwork show of Grand Dukes and Little Dukes, of ministers and courtesans, of all the doubles, marched past before the columns, the

SVD (Kozintsev and Trauberg, 1927)

draperies and the porcelain vases on their mahogany socles. Then, through pretty streets that normally served as decoration for picture postcards, Cossacks galloped, brandishing their whips. Against other picture postcards the crowd ran like operatic extras. In a dungeon, the juvenile, his eyes pathetically blackened with soot, adopted heroic poses while the Queen of the Screen, victim of Tsarism, poured glycerine tears. Each scene was shot three ways: first the whole scene in long shot; then the camera was brought in for medium shots and, very rarely, for close-ups. If the action took place at night the scene was tinted blue; sunny scenes were done in yellow and forest scenes in green.

The very atmosphere of Sevzapkino was in contradiction to the general artistic atmosphere of the times. The people seemed too calm and too commercial. The film-makers lived without urgency, they loved abstract sermons and long reminiscences. They had their professional secrets, but only spoke evasively of them. When they spoke of art it was in lofty tones. But the stories of the scenario scribbled on a cuff during dinner, of the film made by night in the sets of another picture (the studio caretaker having been bribed) sounded much more natural and sincere and human in their mouths. There was nothing here which reminded me of the rehearsals at Mardjanov's or of the burning passions of the painters I knew who could not understand that an artist could have any point of interest in his life other than his work. Here they knew everything, were certain of everything. No one had any doubts.

The people who were working here were settled, unaffected by anything outside administrative hitches. They knew before they began which films make money, and which lose; what does well on the screen and what it is best to leave alone. The total experience of these people, which permitted them to settle everything with such assurance, dated from the pre-revolutionary cinema. Although the organization had changed, the old tastes and the old habits remained. The pre-revolutionary cinema also made films on historico-revolutionary themes. . . . Artistically speaking, Sevzapkino did not yet exist: from end to end it was still pure 'Parisiana'.

Does any influence of FEKS survive today? Generally speaking I think that in art there are certain periods which only bear fruit after many years. And, again, it's not as simple as that! Time can never exactly repeat itself. If what is revived today from the art of the 1920s were exactly like it was before, we would certainly question the usefulness of such a retrogression: epigones are uninteresting. But when experiments like ours, the violent sentiments inspired by contemporary life, can still nourish the work of the young, then it seems to me that that is valuable. In any period man must remain faithful to his own time and to himself. It is bad for someone of sixteen to live as if he were fifty. The greatest happiness is to live at sixteen with all that those sixteen years signify, not to be older than one's own age. And it is equally bad for an older man to try to remain what he was in his youth: to do that is not to be rejuvenated, but to fall back into childishness.

For me the most powerful charm of the 1920s was that the epoch was young, and so were we; our epoch was contained in all that we did. That is important. Notice that what seemed too difficult in all these experiments, what remained inaccessible to the audience of the time, has in succeeding years all become simple and comprehensible. In this connection I would like to recall our first collaboration with Shostakovitch, in 1928. He had written an orchestral score to accompany our silent film, *New Babylon*. The day of the première, in all the cinemas, all the complaints books carried the same protest: 'The conductor of the orchestra was quite drunk tonight.' What had happened was that Shostakovitch had used instrumental combinations so unusual that even the philharmonic orchestras only assimilated them with difficulty. Naturally this unheard-of music baffled the cinema audiences, who blamed the inebriety of the conductor. After only a few years, this same score was accepted as easily as could be: no one now finds it inaccessible. When we talk of the cinema and the audience, we must not consider them as remaining in a static state: the cinema changes, and so does the audience. And what has seemed difficult at a certain period of the cinema soon becomes quite simple and accessible.

The young creators who dreamed of the cinema at that time varied in the degrees of their talent, the sum of their knowledge and their experience of life. Nevertheless this generation was characterized by a common trait: these young people were all absolutely unconcerned with commerce. For them the box-office did not exist. The aesthetic of the commercial film was not only foreign to them but frankly antagonistic. The heritage of the commercial cinema was slight, and of no value to them. Naturally there were people of talent in the studios before the Revolution, and the cinema historians remind us of their films. Even so there was not the very slimmest line of living continuity between the two cinemas. 'Let us not forget that at the beginning of the 1920s we entered the Soviet cinema not as something already existing and formed', wrote Eisenstein. 'We arrived like Bedouins or gold-prospectors. On virgin territory. A land which hid enormous resources of which even now only a ridiculously tiny part has been exploited and cultivated.' 'The directors of my generation who came to the cinema', wrote Dovzhenko later, 'were like the prospectors in Jack London's stories, who, abandoning the places they knew, left for Alaska and dug the sterile rock, in cold and hunger, for a year or two years, in order to discover a seam of gold.' Even if I had not reread these articles, the image of 'prospectors' and above all 'digging the sterile rock' would just the same have appeared in this manuscript. In imagination fantastic treasure glittered, but the place where it was concealed was quite unknown. Still it seemed to us that one blow with the pick would make the gold glitter or the oil leap up towards the sun.

Our first scenario, *The Adventures of Oktyabrina*, was a sort of propaganda film-poster: the influence of the propaganda plays and the Rosta windows shows clearly in every moment of the film. The capitalistic shark has been introduced to Petrograd and demands repayment of the Tsarist debts by the peasants and the workers. The shark wore a silk hat; he was played by Sergei Martinson (whose first role it was), with no make-up apart from enormous black velvet eyebrows. Hearing of the arrival of Coolidge Curzonovitch Poincaré (the name of the shark), the NEP-man, in a fashionable check suit, lets himself go. The plots of this duo are foiled by the young komsomol girl Oktyabrina (played by the dancer Z. Tarakhovskaia). The young girl, wearing a felt hat with a star of the Red Army, puts things to rights, and continues the struggle against survivals of the past. All these characters seemed directly descended from the propaganda lorry which entertained the populace at the May Day parade. It was all rather disconnected, but galloped along on the screen, full of dizzying abridgements of the story and shock cuts. And when the narrative got stuck, letters would appear on the screen: dancing about in the manner of cartoon films, they would group themselves into words, forming slogans that were then familiar.

We tamed the old wild beast with three legs and a great glass eye: an ancient Pathé camera, practically worn out. The handle turned with an asthmatic panting noise. All at once the panting turned to a rattle: something had seized up. The side was opened and out fell the film, concertina'd. But this prehistoric beast seemed to us a miracle. We could hoist its three feet to the highest point in the town and bend its glass eye downwards. We could bury it or stride over it. The handle could turn faster or slower; we could wind back the film and superimpose one, two (five, ten) other images. The dis-

The Adventures of Oktyabrina (Kozintsev and Trauberg, 1925)

Grigori Kozintsev

Grigori Kozintsev (in the late 1950s)

comfort of the places in which we chose to shoot was to play an important part in our destiny. The director assigned to the film, Tchaikowski, listened sympathetically to our ideas but when he discovered that the first shot was to be made on the sloping roof of a very tall building, he declined to be present at the start of shooting. As our next viewpoint was the spire of the Admiralty building, shooting from just below the weather-vane, we found ourselves working alone, without supervision.

'Each of us came to the cinema in his own way and following his own road', wrote Eisenstein on the occasion of the twentieth anniversary of Soviet cinema. 'Here are the chemist, Pudovkin; the teacher, Dovzhenko; me, an engineer; Dzigan whom I still recall as an actor of the Rakhmanov studio; here are Kozintsev, Yutkevitch and Kuleshov come from painting; Alexandrov, a cinema technician, prop man and lighting assistant in the theatre; Ermler, a member of the Cheka; Shengelaya, the poet. . . . And had it not been for the Revolution, who knows if the year 1940 would have united us under the covers of the same album, as men who have had the good fortune and the honour to build the first twenty years of socialist cinema.' What is good is that each one of us participated in this construction in his own fashion, and followed his own path. What is still better is that we all of us felt the community of the effort undertaken. No one worked in isolation; each could hear the pick-axe of his neighbour. Blow after blow, in the most diverse areas, the land ceased to be fallow and barren.

108

7. Sergei Apollinarievitch Gerassimov

Gerassimov sheds further light on the history and methods of the Factory of the Eccentric Actor, which was to make so considerable a contribution of personnel to the new Soviet cinema. Born in 1906, Gerassimov studied painting and then theatre design in Petrograd. Joining FEKS, he entered the cinema as an actor in Kozintsev and Trauberg's *Mishka against Yudenitch* (1925). He continued to work with FEKS until 1930, both as actor and assistant director. After this he split from the group to become a director in his own right. In addition he has often written his own scenarios and played in his own films.

As a professor at the All-Union State Film Institute (VGIK), Gerassimov directs the directors' faculty and also the actors' studio. Over half the most significant post-war directors and actors of the Soviet cinema have been taught by him, notably Sergei Bondarchuk, L. Kulidjanov, Z. Kirienko, T. Lioznova, I. Makarova. Many of these made their first acting appearances in his film *The Young Guard* (1948).

Films: *Twenty-Two Misfortunes* (1930, with S. Bartenev), *The Forest* (1931), *The Heart of Solomon* (1932), *Do I Love You?* (1934), *The Bold Seven* (1936), *Komsomolsk* (1937), *The Teacher* (1939), *Masquerade* (1941), *Film Notes on Battle No. 1* (1941), *The Old Guard* (1941), *The Invincibles* (1941, with Mikhail Kalatozov), *Cine-concert for the 25th Anniversary of the Red Army* (1943, with Kalatozov and Efim Dzigan), *The Great Earth* (1944), *The Young Guard* (1948), *Liberated China* (1950), *Country Doctor* (1951), *Nadezda* (1954), *Quiet Flows the Don* (1957–8), *The Sputnik Speaks* (1959, with E. Volk, V. Dorman and G. Oganissian), *Men and Beasts* (1962), *The Journalist* (1967).

Out of the Factory of the Eccentric Actor

If I must speak of my biography, which really began, like those of a number of my *confrères*, in the 1920s, I clearly must begin by talking about FEKS. It was an undertaking of young – very young – people. I was seventeen. Kozintsev was eighteen and seemed very mature to me. People of twenty were 'masters' to us, 'old ones', rich in experience, belonging almost to another generation.

But to begin at the beginning. I was born on 21 May 1906 in a village near Cheliabinsk, on the Ural. Being born in the country has played a part in my life, for the impressions of my childhood have never left me. The region where I was born is one of the most curious and picturesque in the country. The peasants, Ural Cossacks, have tremendous character and are remarkably interesting people. I went to school in Sverdlovsk, then, at fourteen, had to start work to assist my family. So I went into a factory. But soon, following the advice of my brother who thought I had a gift for painting, I left for Leningrad to enrol in the School of Fine Arts. There it was that I got to know comrades who belonged to FEKS. They spoke to me about their group, told me that there was an experimental studio where young people sought to create a 'New Art'. I had always been attracted by the theatre, even more than by painting. I loved to act in front of the mirror, to play the roles from my favourite plays, in particular Schiller's Franz Moor, though God knows why.

Still pursuing my studies at the School of Fine Arts, I enrolled, almost keeping it secret from myself, in the company of actors of the experimental theatre directed by Vsevolodsky-Gerngross. They experimented in spectacles derived from folk traditions. I made a few appearances on the stage, or more precisely in the arena, done up in a venerable beard, in the mute role of a wedding guest. These were my débuts as an actor. I thought then that it was perhaps my true vocation. At the time I had no real passion for painting (nowadays I have!), but in any event the painting classes proved useful later on. One day, a friend in the School of Fine Arts proposed, 'How about coming and doing a few somersaults?'

I had already been some time in the capital, but embarrassed to admit my provincial ignorance, I refrained from questions as to what such a thing or such an expression might mean. In general I blindly followed my friends, preferring to learn as I went on. Needless to say these experiences were not always entirely beneficial to my formation; but this time my friend's peculiar invitation was truly to decide my destiny.

He took me to number 2, Proletkult Street, where FEKS was then operating. (Only later was I to decipher the meaning of that enigmatic little word.*) There, on the sixth floor, in a huge room, a score of youngsters of my own age were performing somersaults under the direction of two masters, the older of whom, Leonid Trauberg, was twenty-one. Grigori Kozintsev was scarcely eighteen, but his authority over this rowdy crew was already absolute and without appeal.

At this first meeting, curiously enough, Kozintsev talked to me about the FEKS' intention of producing *Hamlet*. Then, after having put me through a summary examination, he declared that I might suit the principal role – so long as I understood and accepted the artistic principles of his group, principles which he at once explained to me, at least as far as it concerned the future production of *Hamlet*.

FEKS rejected, overthrew and negated in every possible way pre-existing forms of theatrical art. To this effect, its members possessed a whole arsenal of whistles and rattles which allowed them to organize demonstrations in the 'academic' theatres.† The programme of the group was set out in a little booklet with a very alluring cover: in large type was written: 'Allez hup! Eccentric Parade!' and as epigraph, in smaller type, the motto of FEKS: 'It's better to be a young pup than an old bord of Paradise – Mark Twain.'

I joined them with joy. In this workshop they were doing absolutely unimaginable things! The avowed end of our activity was the overthrow of all the old values. We denied everything (including ourselves sometimes) in manifestos as fiery as definitive. The team consisted of interesting young people, all ardent and sincere. We had contacts with Mayakovski and his

---

* Fabrika Eksentricheskovo (Aktera): Factory of the Eccentric (Actor).

† For the young the term 'academic' even covered the constructivist productions of the Kamerny Theatre.

Gerassimov in *The Devil's Wheel* (Kozintsev and Trauberg, 1926)

'LEF' group. Meyerhold also played a role in our group. We made a lot of racket, but we were so young that people accepted us cheerfully: they are just kids who want to do something! What? They don't yet know a thing themselves.

Still the productions we mounted were not without their interest. *Vnechtorg* on the Eiffel Tower*, *Hamlet* completely 'reworked'. The modernization began with the death of the King. Death reached him through the ear, but he succumbed not to a démodé poison, but to a high-tension electric current through a telephone receiver. This spectacle never saw the light of day. Nevertheless we had already learned the texts of Kozintsev and Trauberg, written after the manner of Maurice Leblanc and Gaston Leroux.

Then the cinema came and swept us off our feet. We were all of us precipitated into this path which, it (rightly) seemed to us, offered a much vaster field and richer means to express ourselves. I did not take part in the first film made by FEKS, *The Adventures of Oktyabrina*, because of illness. But I participated very fully in the second.

Mishka against Yudenitch was an improbable sort of muddle in which it was impossible to know what was what. The whole scenario was written on a little scrap of paper; everything had to be improvised in the course of shooting, and we might – had to – do anything that came into our heads. This adventure passed all imagining, and, when I think back to it, I tell myself that only our robust good health saved us from certain death. Regardless of the weather we performed clad only in football slips. We leapt from signals on to moving trains; we galloped along railway tracks, breaking the legs of the horses – and our own. It was an accumulation of the most audacious tricks, dizzy falls, the maddest inventions.

The film was presented in a very small theatre, before a public that was utterly dumbfounded. Since then no one has looked at it again . . . I don't think it will take a place in the history of the Soviet cinema!

At that time we had already moved into a mansion on Gagarinskaya Street – we had inherited it from the merchant Elisseev. As well as Gobelins tapestries, there still remained some bits of furniture and a gigantic red carpet (the famous six by eighteen metre carpet) which cost us the trouble of a weekly cleaning. Because on it we did all our apprenticeship – gymnastics, acrobatics, boxing – vital disciplines of the actor's profession.

The theoretical part of the training fell to Leonid Trauberg. He did his job with a passion and an extraordinary mastery, conveying to us with immense fervour all the artistic and literary discoveries he had accumulated in his twenty-two years. Grigori Kozintsev taught the principal matter, called 'cine-gesture'. It was based on the mathematical precision of American comic and detective films. The actor was required not to 'feel'. The very word 'feeling' was only ever pronounced with derisive grimaces accompanied by scornful laughter from the whole troupe.

---

* Vnechtorg: abbreviation of Vnechnaia Torgovlia – exterior commerce.

Gerassimov in *Mishka against Yudenitch* (Kozintsev and Trauberg, 1925); and (right) *The Overcoat* (Kozintsev and Trauberg, 1926)

By every possible means, honest or not, we procured posters for the adventure films which at that time swept our screens. We papered the walls of the Elisseev mansion with them, and everything that was acted between those walls exactly corresponded to the spirit and to the form of these highly coloured pictures of ferocious heroes with pistols in their hands, and masked blonde beauties. These were the origins of the cinema which, ten years later was to produce Kozintsev and Trauberg's great *Maxim* trilogy. . . .

This sort of dementia lasted until the appearance of Eisenstein's *Strike*. The director was – officially – our true chief. He was all of twenty-four years old and for us an old man. We always said, 'The Old Man says . . .', 'The Old Man thinks that. . . .' But Kozintsev remained our undisputed *master*. And I recall how after having seen *Strike*, he came back to the studio rather thoughtful, and said: 'All that we've been doing up to now is baby stuff. We have to review our whole fashion of thinking, everything. We have to look for serious links with real life.' And from then on the whole group set itself to read, to argue, to study seriously.

We were then infatuated with the American cinema. Detective films, burlesques, melodramas and of course all the films of Griffith were for us revelations and models. More exactly, we were inspired to re-do them better, according to our own fashion. So, emerging from the eccentric period, we

115

The Devil's Wheel

fell into the detective melodrama style. This stage was quickly passed, and there soon began to appear new elements, more appropriate to the nascent Soviet cinema. We grew up. We became more lucid, more conscientious. The most important moment of FEKS's activity was *The New Babylon*, inspired by Zola and already a part of the patrimony of our cinematography. From this film dates our transition from the eccentric cinema to the political cinema.

Then – or rather a little before this time – we had all become profoundly influenced by certain monuments of literature: Zola, Gogol. . . . (We had made a film adaptation of *The Overcoat*.) *The Devil's Wheel* clearly showed the influence of writers like Tynianov and Shklovski, that is, the formalist school of literature of Leningrad. This whole *pléiade* of erudite, intelligent and rather exceptional men taught us that life is never quite simple. And it was from the shock of these influences, contradictory as they often were, that our conception of the world – and also the first glimmerings of cinema realism – were born.

The first film to bring some notoriety to our group was *SVD* (the Society for the Great Cause). It was the first film in which human and social elements and historic problems at last appeared. Then came *The New Babylon* – an enormous success and a true 'problem' film, which spoke of the Paris Commune and evoked life in France in 1870. By now it was already 1928;

Gerassimov in *Alone* (Kozintsev and Trauberg, 1931)

we were all around twenty-two years old and felt ourselves rich with all the wisdom and all the experience in the world. As, despite our success, we had to keep our studio going, we sub-let part of it to a certain Klementi Mintz, a young man just sixteen years old, who was already directing his own studio, named Stumazit* – and even now I cannot decipher the meaning of this formula. . . . One day by accident, we heard the instruction which the young leader of Stumazit was giving his disciples: he said that one of the immediate aims of the group was the demolition of FEKS, 'that academic institution'. So we learned how old we had become!

We approached the sound film with few preconceptions. Eisenstein, Alexandrov and Pudovkin had just issued a declaration affirming that the sound film must not talk, at risk of losing its specific qualities of an international art. The Great Silent Cinema had to remain, if not totally aphonic, at least without articulated language. Over this there were great polemics! . . . We now know that this manifesto has been refuted by subsequent events. But at the time we saw profound truth in it. And our first tentative sound film, *Alone*, in 1931, employed only the music of Shostakovitch with, here and there, scraps of insignificant phrases, fragments of speech introduced by

---

* Stumazit: Studia Massovych Zrelichtch i Torjestv (Studio of Spectacles and Mass Festivals.)

Alone

chance without any discernible reason. But before that, at the time of *The New Babylon*, we sought the possibility of accompanying a film with music strictly and organically linked to the action. At the time Shostakovitch was associated with our group: for *The New Babylon* he wrote a score which obligatorily had to accompany every projection of the film – generally, as was the fashion, on piano. It would be very interesting, I think, to be able to study this early work of Shostakovitch (he was then eighteen) today.

As for myself, I continued my career as an actor. Up to the arrival of sound, the actor blindly followed the will of the director. There was no question of departing from the character as the director conceived it. I was one of these actors, and, little by little, I felt rising within me a sense of revolt against the system. I wanted to do something else, according to my own ideas: I did not want to be told any more how to do every gesture, every expression. I was then first assistant to Kozintsev and Trauberg, on *Alone*, and also playing the part of the kolkhoz chairman, an obtuse and stupid bureaucrat. I recalled my childhood in the country, and I saw that the text for my role did not in any respect correspond to reality. And I did not want to play an invented person, a creation of the imagination, but a real, living man whom I had really known for myself. And so it was that in this silent film (it was shot silent) I began to talk. Really. To pronounce phrases which had meaning, which helped me to identify myself with my character. This – instead of simply miming the movement of the lips, as was then good form – actually to speak, to pronounce real words was considered in very bad taste. From that moment, I think, dated my first real relationship with art. The first glimmer of that relationship, anyway. Moreover, it is from this film that my path took a different turn from that of FEKS: this was our last work together.

Earlier I had undertaken to direct my first film, *Twenty-Two Misfortunes*, from a scenario by the writer Skorinko. A real disaster! I collaborated on it with Bartenev, whose first effort it also was. We were both of us spectacularly ignorant in the matter of *mise en scène*, and were allied in the enterprise for reasons which were very obscure. The film turned out as weak in sense as in talent and, thank heaven, no fragment of it survives today.

Then, alone this time, I made *The Forest*, a film with actors, about the life of woodcutters. There must have seemed some hope in me, because people in my crew began to say: 'This one'll be a director one day.' At the same time the film marked my first steps on the thorny road of screen-writing. I must admit that I have always been very attracted by this literary exercise: I think I get most pleasure out of writing. This was in 1931, and from this point can be traced a more or less continuous line in my work. *Do I Love You?* was still a silent film even though the first talking pictures (Ekk's *Road to Life*, etc.) had already come out. But up to 1935 I was only trusted with silent subjects, to limit the possible havoc!

My first talking picture was *The Bold Seven* which I wrote in collaboration with the novelist Guerman. My serious biography as a true director begins

Komsomolsk (Gerassimov, 1937)

with this film. It is the first film made in my own style. I had always been irritated by the intrusion of theatrical methods into the cinema. All those forced intonations, that fashion of playing to the public, facing the camera and the microphone, all the other borrowings from the theatre which marked the early sound period, seemed to me of heart-breaking naivety. And Guerman and I resolved to make our first talking picture a sort of protest against all these bad habits. We wanted to try to give the impression of people spied on by the camera, something specifically cinematographic. This 'direct' vision even now remains an ideal style which some achieve and others do not. So you see that little has changed. Basically, the things we seek are the same, with each one undertaking the search according to his own ideas.

The Bold Seven brought me considerable success, which, I may say, rather alarmed me, because for my own part I could not see in it any element of that 'discovery' with which I was credited. For me this way of making films was simply the natural one. Still, I perceived a certain self-discovery. Immediately after this I made *Komsomolsk*, which continued in the same direction, with the same actors, upon whom I exercised my talents as an educator. Kozintsev had from the start got me into this habit of cinematographic teaching, by entrusting the direction of his studio to me during his absences. So *The Bold*

Seven marks the début of my pedagogic career: the unit was essentially my class, my pupils.

And I have remained a teacher. First of all in my workshop in the Leningrad Studios; then, since the war, in Moscow where, in my course at the All-Union State Institute of Cinematography (VGIK) I have formed four generations of students among whom have been some extremely interesting actors and directors. That is the essence of my work during the twenty years of my life in Moscow.

The Creative Process

As concerns creative methods in the cinema I have ideas which may seem to you extremist, in any event polemic in origin. I consider that the cinema, despite its label as a 'synthetic' art, despite its reputation as a team activity, is absolutely and rigorously, and against every contrary appearance, an author's art. Who is the author? The question comes up every time that there is a failure – or a success! In my view the author is the one who intellectually dominates the ensemble. It can be the writer, the director, the cameraman, the actor. It is always the one who is the real master of the initial idea and of the *passions* of the work. The one who literally dominates the others. Sometimes an odd thing happens: someone begins a film and, in the end, the author is not he, but someone else. Often it is the actor who becomes the author of the film, and it can even happen that the composer comes along and overwhelms all to become the true author.

Creation is a struggle of forces. The best result occurs when all the forces are concentrated in the hands of a single person. When the director of the film, while having a plastic vision of his work, can be the cameraman at the same time as he is actor, and while his taste and his knowledge permit him to dominate the music. Then the true cinema is born: *when the author is one person.* When he has in his head the whole scoring of a film in a single, achieved entity. . . . Yes, for me the cinema remains an author's art, not a team art. In this way Eisenstein and Dovzhenko worked; in this way Chaplin and Fellini work. Whatever the scenarists may say about it, the author of the film must find himself at the very source of the work. The cinema is not an interpretative art, but an art of genesis.

When I have adapted works of literature, I have never considered them as *my* films. *Quiet Flows the Don* is Sholokhov's film. I have often been criticized for not having reformed the novel to make a Gerassimov film from it. That has always infuriated me: my problem was exactly that of subordinating myself entirely to author Sholokhov. I loved and love that novel far too much not to want to respect it scrupulously, to betray nothing of its spirit and its essence and its form, so that the spectator sees quite simply the book which has come to life in the cinema. Why should I want to trample the spoils of the living Sholokhov, as some people have wished I had done? I had the same problems when I adapted Lermontov's drama *Masquerade* in 1941. I have always loved Lermontov, who comes next to Pushkin in my preferences,

Masquerade (Gerassimov, 1941)

perhaps because of certain romantic traditions which derive from Schiller. I adapted *Masquerade* with all the delight of a gourmet faced with his favourite dish; but there, too, I tried only to reproduce what Lermontov had created. There is a theatrical tradition of having Arbenin, the jealous husband and murderer, played by septuagenarians, although he is in fact at the most twenty-six. And I made a youthful *Masquerade*, a story of young people, not something from a theatrical museum. The one question I never ceased to ask myself was 'How would Lermontov himself have wanted to see this?' And it was the same with *The Young Guard*: the author Fadeyev was a very close friend; I knew all his thoughts, the deeper reasons behind each episode. So ... these are cases in which I voluntarily cede the title of author to the one who really is author. The author is the one who is strongest.

One last remark. At the moment there is much talk about de-dramatization. De-dramatization, as I conceive it, is simply the rejection of the classical rules of dramaturgy in favour of the dramaturgy of real life. To depart from mechanical methods, tricks of the trade; to move towards the comprehension, the interpretation of real facts, things which actually exist in life, in all their complexity and all their contradictions – this is how I understand the new dramaturgy. Inevitably it involves a kind of rupture, the destruction of the traditional form with all its obligatory elements: exposition of the theme, development of the action, progressive dramatic build-up, culmination and dénouement. . . . This sort of 'sonata form' structure is never met with in real life, and by consequence must be abandoned. I am all for life, because life confounds art. It is so much more interesting!

Life must be more powerful than art and, of all the arts, the cinema is nearest to life. Pudovkin even used to say that therein lies its poverty and its nakedness. From its infancy the cinema has been accustomed to depict certain fragments of life within the narrow limits of the screen, within the screen's very precise frame. This is an error. You must not limit yourself to depicting the elements of the action within a given frame. You must have a sense of the liberty which exists beyond the frame, 'out of shot'. You must have, and convey, the feeling of life effervescing on either side of the screen. You must give the impression that the screen is only a window open upon an immense life. All action strictly imprisoned within the perimeter of the screen, narrowed down to this flat and shut-in plane belongs to a cinema of tableau-makers for whom I have the most violent repugnance. For me the true, right way is that which leads from the documentary cinema to the cinema of *mise en scène*. Yes, that is my own little idea of things.

(Recorded in Paris, May 1964)

Pudovkin in *A Living Corpse* (Otsep, 1929) and in *The Happy Canary* (Kuleshov, 1929)

8. Vsevolod Illarionovitch Pudovkin

The rather formal and turgid jargon of official aesthetic debate tends to obscure Pudovkin's assessment of the creative moment when a whole generation of young artists discovered in the cinema the means to express all the excitement they felt in the new society that had been created around them.

Pudovkin, born in 1893 – a year before Dovzhenko and five before Eisenstein – was the oldest of the enchanted first generation of the Soviet cinema. He studied at the Physics and Mathematical Faculty at Moscow; served at the front (1914–15), was taken prisoner, escaped and came back to Moscow in 1918. The following year he entered VGIK and worked on Gardin's *Sickle and Hammer* – the first Soviet feature film – as actor and assistant director. Joining Kuleshov's studio he worked on and in *The Strange Adventures of Mr West in the Land of the Bolsheviks* and *The Death Ray*. In 1925 he directed a short, *Chess Fever*, and later the same year made a remarkable scientific documentary on Pavlov's experiments, *Mechanism of the Brain*. The following year saw the release of his masterpiece, an adaptation of Gorki's *Mother*. Two more films of incontestable greatness, *The End of St Petersburg* (1927) and *Storm Over Asia* (1928) were followed by the somewhat disappointing *A Simple Case* (1930). After joining with Eisenstein and Alexandrov in their manifesto on the sound film, Pudovkin made his own first sound film, boldly experimental in its techniques, *Deserter* (1933). None of his sound films, however, ever achieved the supreme success of his great silent works. His subsequent films were: *Victory* (1938), *Minin and Podjarsky* (1939), *Suvorov* (1940), *Twenty Years of Cinema* (1940, with Esther Shub), *The Feast at Jirmunka* (in *Film Notes on Battle No. 6*), *The Murderers Are on the Road* (1942, not released), *In the Name of the Fatherland* (1943, with Dmitri Vassiliev), *Admiral Nakhimov* (1946), *Three Meetings* (1948; one episode; the others were directed by Yutkevitch and A. Ptushko), *Zhukovsky* (1950, with Dmitri Vassiliev), *The Return of Vassili Bortnikov* (1953).

Pudovkin died 30 June 1953.

The Force of Poetry

The creative success of an artist is a highly complex phenomenon. It would be a serious error to suppose that such success is conditioned by the narrow circle of the circumstances and the events of his personal life. We know that the greatest scientific discoveries – just like the creation of the greatest works of art – are inevitably linked to a certain general tension of human thought, directed in a precise orientation. The birth of such a work is produced as if in an incandescent atmosphere which arrives at the critical temperature where, like a sudden deflagration, the chemical reaction produces a new quality. And like the blinding light and the thunder which suddenly render visible and audible the electric tension accumulated in the clouds, the great work of art, in a powerful discharge, expresses what was in process of being born, growing, and accumulating force in thousands of human brains.

I remember when I was still in school, in 1910, and Halley's comet was to break into the terrestrial orbit. According to the calculations of the astronomers, the collision of the two celestial bodies was inevitable. People were overwhelmed by the prospect. Moscow prepared itself for something rather like the end of the world. The worry was quite serious, because it was known that the comet carried with it a noxious gas which killed every living thing. The enormity of the event excited me and overwhelmed me in the extreme. Tomorrow, yes, tomorrow something was going to happen which had never happened before, of which no one really knew the exact nature. And I was to be a witness of it.

Of course my efforts to formulate today what my feelings were at that time can only feebly translate their true substance. My sentiments and my thoughts were then confused and lacked precision, but one thing I am certain about: the quest for the new, for the unforeseen, for the unknown was always in me and has not diminished right up to today. It is precisely that tendency which drew me to science, while my passion for art arises from a natural inclination to find expression for the dreams which wandered in me.

When I encountered the cinema for the first time, it struck my imagination by the particularity of its problems. No other art was quite like it. I must have felt it intuitively, because my new passion was sudden and powerful.

Abandoning the factory where I was working as a chemist, I enrolled as a pupil of Kuleshov, a young director whose work was subsequently to provide a point of departure for the Soviet cinema. We remember this period very well, linked as it was to the foundation of our socialist State as well as to the birth and the expansion of our cinema. The great struggle of an entire people was refreshed by the highest ideas of a universal significance. The best of our films from this epoch are known everywhere. All bore the stamp of the different style of each individual author, yet they possessed a common quality: each aspired to unite in a convincing narrative events which were spread over wide intervals of time and an enormous area of terrestrial space. In revealing the essence of great humanist ideas, they tended not to relate the links existing between different phenomena, but to *show* those links, visually, with all the persuasive force of the thing which can be seen at a glance. Only the cinema could permit this, and with such power.

Sergei Eisenstein's *The Battleship Potemkin* appeared at the moment when the best among the pre-revolutionary intellectuals were being profoundly affected by all the great and the new things which were brought into life by the victorious working class. In art, the traditions of the past were engaged in a merciless struggle with the ideas of people who had linked their art with the work of the proletariat – ideas still not fully formulated, but directed towards a unique and precise end.

The old and familiar artistic methods crumbled and collapsed. As for the new ways, they were primarily proclaimed in the fire of polemic, in which it was sometimes forgotten that only their realization could resolve the debate. The lives of those artists who failed to find in themselves the strength and the courage to reject the weight of the commonplace and of the old habits, pined away in obscure corners. In literature Vladimir Mayakovski, already firmly entrenched, made his powerful voice heard above the shouting and tumult of the battle. In the art of the cinema, the new, while waiting for its turn, was revealed in purely formal research. Lev Kuleshov forced us to acquire visual taste and taught us the ABC of montage. Eisenstein himself contributed to the tentative efforts to find a new direction through pure form. In *Strike*, the clandestine meeting of workers moves into the water and under an old pinnace. Only because it was very unexpected and strange, although not very likely. . . .

Vsevolod Pudovkin

The extreme tension of the theoretical polemic made the atmosphere very heated. Innumerable hotheads had the same powerful conviction: above all an artist must seek a large and *poetic* significance in the world around him. This law is not dead, and never will die in art, because it is precisely this which expresses the difference between art and the other fields of human creation. In works of art, the victorious class wishes always to see the pathetic grandeur of its historic struggle.

And, with the scenarist Nina Agadjanova, Eisenstein tackled an immense and new theme. He wished to show in a film all the grandeur and all the pathos of the revolutionary struggle of 1905. As must inevitably happen, everything contributed to help him. His own enormous talent, the freshness of his powers, still intact, the enthusiasm of his comrades impassioned by the common effort, and above all, I repeat, this general atmosphere of creative tension, still undisclosed but already existing and demanding a discharge. And the discharge followed. It was thunder and lightning.

In a flash of lightning, the thunder overwhelmed the audiences of our own country, rolled over Europe, reached even to America, and returned to us in the echo of vast applause.

Glory and honour to the artist who was able, even if only partially, to absorb in his conscience the thoughts and the common sentiments of all his people. Such a creator can be justly proud of a real artistic success.

129

The End of St Petersburg (Pudovkin, 1927)

9. Anatoli Dimitrievitch Golovnya

With his unembarrassed pride in his and Pudovkin's achievements; his forthright criticisms of other artists; his random knocks at critics in general; his mistrust of Eisenstein's 'intellectualizing' in *October*; his rather rigid views on education; his conviction that if *The Seven Samurai* were shown in the Soviet Union it would lead to orgies of knife-fighting – Golovnya is not the most attractive figure in this collection of cinema artists. Still there is no question of the value of his vivid self-portrait, representing as he does the incorrigible old campaigner, committed to a conventional, conservative position, which probably echoes a majority voice among the influential middle-aged of Soviet art.

Like Pudovkin, Golovnya was somewhat older than most of the first-generation directors. He was born on 2 February 1900. From 1919 to 1922 he was examining magistrate at Kherson. In 1925 he graduated from the Cameramen's Faculty of Moscow, met Pudovkin and began a collaboration that lasted throughout Pudovkin's life (*Chess Fever, Mechanics of the Brain, Mother, End of St Petersburg, Storm Over Asia, Deserter, Victory, Minin and Podjarsky, Suvorov, The Feast at Jirmunka, Admiral Nakhimov, Zhukovsky*). Regarded, along with Tisse and Andrei Moskvin, as one of the founders of the Soviet school of cinematography, Golovnya also worked with Obolensky (*Little Bricks*, 1925), Protazanov (*The Restaurant Man*, 1927), Otzep (*The Living Corpse*, 1929), V. Petrov (*The Elusive Ivan*, 1943).

Golovnya also directed several films – *Bread* (1930), *Fish* (1930), *The Great Everyday* (1932) – and wrote the screenplay of V. Nemoliayev's *Rudy's Career* (1934). He is Professor at VGIK, where he is in charge of the Cameramen's Faculty; and has written several theoretical works on the cinema.

132

Broken Cudgels

The Beginnings of the Soviet cinema. To understand how an art was created at this time, it is first necessary to understand that it was achieved by men who had just created a new social order. I had fought for a fair number of years – in the First World War and then during the whole of the Civil War which had involved me in quite enough battles. Pudovkin was taken prisoner in 1915. He was seriously wounded, and had a huge scar on his arm. He was interned in East Prussia for three years, escaped in 1917 and took eight months to get to Moscow. When he arrived there, he discovered a new world, new men and new human relationships.

When we began our work in the cinema, we wanted to incarnate in our films the reason why we had fought.

Then also it must be remembered that we had no authority over us. That was a quite astonishing thing! Personally I am of the opinion that it is parents who bring up their children best. But an alternative possibility is not excluded: it may be that children bring themselves up very well. As long as they possess a certain ardour, a thirst for life. That was the atmosphere in which we worked – everyone was looking for a new direction. Pudovkin sought new directions. So did Eisenstein, and all of us with them. There was no pressure on us.

That was the atmosphere. The best that can exist for artists. Nobody said *how* we must do things. Today it is notorious that every critic knows how a film should be made. The only ones who don't know are the director and the cameraman. First-year students know better than anyone else. In the third year they don't know it any longer, of course, but on entering VGIK no one is in any doubt about anything.

Chess Fever (Pudovkin, 1925)

Pudovkin and I got to know each other in the following fashion. I was a student in the newly opened Cinema Technical School. I was the first student of the first year of the first course. During the summer they sent us for practical work in the studios. I happened to get into Kuleshov's technical team, under the cameraman Levitsky. It was in 1924. They were making *The Death Ray* and so I met Pudovkin who was playing the principal role and also acting as co-director. During the work we became very friendly. For our respective biographies, it is worth noting that there were two reasons for this.

At that time a camera was the culmination and summit of all perfection for me. We were shooting in a swamp, a peat-bog. Pudovkin and Fogel had to wade across it. The cameraman Levitsky had placed his camera full in the water. As in any peat-bog, the water was warmish on the surface but icy below. The weather was very changeable, and for that reason two or three hours went by between two takes. And I, devoted assistant that I was, stayed there, in the swamp, holding the camera in position. Pudovkin told me later that he had been fascinated to see a man capable of such patience. Like a great good faithful dog. This was the first incident that made him think it might be worth employing this young man.

He told me about another impression. One day there was a discussion about contemporary art. At that time, as may be imagined, an assistant operator was a mere nobody, no better than a schoolboy. Well, I'd finished the

The Death Ray (Kuleshov, 1925)

gymnasium. . . . During the discussion I gave forth a few opinions which surprised Pudovkin by the knowledge they revealed.

I had also become friendly with other members of our outfit, which abounded with talented people. Such as Leonid Obolensky, who directed the first film on which I was cameraman, *Little Bricks* – a man with a very interesting history.* He must be getting along in years now, I think he is older than me. . . . When Pudovkin was to make his first film, *Mechanism of the Brain*, he asked me to join his unit. And since I am by nature a faithful dog, we continued to work together.

He was a man of great talent. A difficult character, it is true, but that never concerned me. He was extremely nervy and excitable, but when we were working together we got on without any arguments or fights. He was the

---

* Prince Obolensky (b. 1902) studied in the 'pages corps', then broke entirely with his upbringing to enlist in the Red Army. After the Civil War he became a pupil of Kuleshov, proved himself an actor of talent and a fine film-maker. He taught at VGIK until the war. In 1941 he enrolled in the volunteers, was captured and deported to Yugoslavia. Obolensky escaped, sheltered in an orthodox convent, and a year later became a monk. When the Soviet Army arrived, he was arrested for desertion and condemned to several years' forced labour in one of the big construction sites in Siberia. No sooner was he there than he formed a group of film-makers and amateur actors and made a remarkable documentary on the work on which he was employed. Released again, he organized cinema study groups in the region. In 1965 he was director of the documentary studios at Tcheliabinsk, on the Ural.

director and I was the cameraman. He concerned himself with the expression on the face of an actor, and I with the image of the actor which appeared on the screen.

My relations with Pudovkin were thus established. *Mechanism of the Brain* was our school, and it was on this film that we learned and assimilated montage methods. The experiments which we had to film demanded minute examination of visual details, and logical continuity in the exposition of the subject.

The principal subject of the film was Pavlov's dogs. Their reflexes were excited either by bells or by the shadow of food, and in both cases the dogs salivated. Every detail had to be shown in close-up; any longer shot would not give the desired results. Everything had to be precise and clear. Having worked together on this film we ended by forming a regular team. Pudovkin continued to maintain absolute trust in his cameraman when it came to composing a shot.

Generally Pudovkin concentrated principally on work with the actors. No one respected actors like Pudovkin. Whether an actor pleased him or not, or worked to his taste or not. He understood that the actor is the incarnation of the character on the screen, the sole incarnation for the spectator, and that the mood of the actor is crucial. Pudovkin revealed enormous tact in working with his actors. It was most striking with Alexei Denisovich Dikii, on *Admiral Nakhimov*. Dikii was an expansive man, very Russian. Nor did he have any distaste for the bottle. . . . And being a director as well, he had his own ideas on the way things should be done. Pudovkin cried over it sometimes – literally, somewhere in a corner. Yet at the same time, what efforts! Not just to achieve his own ends, but to give Dikii himself the *desire* to play the character as Pudovkin saw him. This was Pudovkin's great accomplishment – without ever constricting the actor, to get him to think in the same way as the director himself.

Or again, take an actor like Cherkassov, who played the role of Suvorov. A man of astonishing talent, and very original, but unlucky and also rather inclined to drink. All this made him terribly vulnerable. And one simply had to see the infinite pains which Pudovkin took to protect him. He made us equally attentive. If the actor were annoyed by a light – then we cut at once. If a collar irritated him, then the costume was changed. If he did not take to someone on the set, then that someone was sent away and a pretty girl brought to take his place.

Now don't forget that Pudovkin was himself an astonishing actor. If you were in the place of one of the actors, and looked at Pudovkin standing beside the camera, you would have seen everything the actor did as if in a mirror. Pudovkin was a very expressive mimic. Moreover he was entirely absorbed in what was happening (which is inevitable, by the way, for any real director). He completely let himself go, inside; and it was this that allowed him to seek, with the actor, the emotional truth of the character. But he never restricted an actor by asking him to copy him, as some directors

Cherkassov in *Suvorov* (Pudovkin, 1941)

do. He sought the truth of the image in the actor, not in himself.

To come back to our débuts: working conditions at that time were particularly difficult. The working method which Pudovkin wished to establish was quite unknown, except perhaps to myself; and Pudovkin had to get the actors used to it. They had to be taught to play not whole scenes, but separate sequences. Consequently he was entirely absorbed by this task and simply had not time to occupy himself with the cameraman's work. And he knew that he had at his side someone who would do exactly what he needed.

The hardest thing to film is the expression on the face of an actor in close-up. It is much harder than any huge crowd scene. That is why a good director busies himself with the actors while the cameraman is nervously struggling to get on film what the actor is doing. He thinks of that and not about his own lighting effects. Nowadays we see a lot of films in which there are more camera effects than effective acting!

Pudovkin began to make *A Simple Case* with the scenarist Rjeshevski. I was opposed to it. We did not have a row; we simply went our separate ways. He worked on *A Simple Case* and I began to make what were then known as 'cultural films'. The first was about the 'Giant' sovkhoz, the first big sovkhoz established in the virgin lands. The film was simply called *Bread*. Then I made another, *Fish*, about fishing co-operatives. That could have been a very interesting film, but as it was already 1931, and the principle of the co-operative had already been supplanted by collectivization, I could not do as much with my film as I had hoped. Those are my own most significant films as a director. I made others subsequently, also in 1930–1. Then I made a feature film, *The Great Everyday*. It was about a peasant who comes to the production line of the Stalingrad tractor factory. But as technology was moving tremendously fast then, by the time the film came out events had passed it by; along with others of the same kind, the film is forgotten now. By that time Pudovkin had finished with his experiments and come back to the kind of film I liked. And we went off together to make *Deserter*.

I had not liked *A Simple Case* because I am a cameraman and used to seeing on the screen what is found in front of the camera. When I am given an unlimited quantity of adjectives instead of a scenario, I no longer know how to go about filming it.

Rjeshevski's script would read: 'A certain marvellous man on some marvellous river side.' I said to the writer: 'Listen! Pudovkin may know who this marvellous man is. But *how* he is marvellous, and how the river side is marvellous – that *I've* got to know, because I'm responsible for it. I don't know what is marvellous about it. As cameraman I cannot be responsible for translating to the screen "A certain marvellous land. . . ." What's marvellous about it?'

I am a concrete and practical man. If you have read my book, you know my respect for literary epithets, imagery and in general the whole of an author's literary means. I have filmed Gorki, and I know what his work expresses! But an incalculable number of adjectives expresses nothing. That is why I refused to do this scenario. Pudovkin did it with another cameraman, and no good came of it – nor could. These 'emotional scenarios' have never succeeded and never will. Rjeshevski was a writer who appropriated all that was worst in Leonid Andreyev and Isaac Babel – both writers of genuine originality – and ended up by being a caricature of both of them.

The 'close-up time' effect which Pudovkin tried out in this film is a very interesting process. Once we made an experimental fragment together, showing the cutting of grass. When we shot at normal speed we simply got an ordinary image of a job of work. When we speeded up the camera and so slowed down the action on the screen, the grass fell slo-o-o-owly! The dewdrops which fell from the heads produced an altogether new and extraordinary spectacle.

Similarly when I was filming the surf. A wave at normal speed comes too fast to be alarming; but if you shoot it in slow motion, you see this great mass advancing, advancing on you. You get quite a different effect.

Pudovkin regarded this purely visual effect as an extension of the expressive means of the cinema. And he wanted to apply the same effect to people. He was then working with 'types' – non-professional actors who had certain characteristics in their mime – the smile for instance – which lent themselves to the same extension of the time of a movement. What is the best thing about

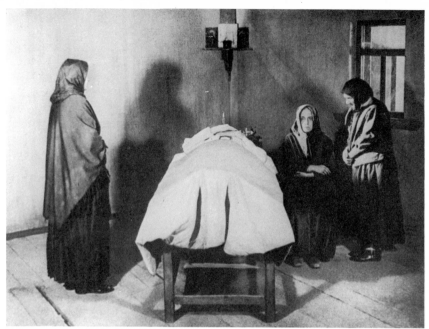

Mother (Pudovkin, 1926)

a person? His smile. By shooting it in slow motion the pleasing effect is prolonged and emphasized. That is Pudovkin's 'magnifying glass of time' which he used in his film *A Simple Case*. Used discreetly, as in *Storm Over Asia* (where he decomposed a fist blow: a retarded movement of the body, followed by an accelerated impact) it can be a good method, increasing the expressive possibilities of the cinema. And if it to some degree complicates the shooting process, all I can say is that I don't know any *simple* process.

To come on to the manifesto against the talking cinema which Eisenstein, Pudovkin and Alexandrov published in 1928, I must say that I feel it the least serious aspect of their careers. It was not a matter of an artistic credo, but the result of imperfect knowledge of sound films. Talking to Pudovkin later, when he had been able to digest the technique and prospects of sound, it was quite clear that the ideas expounded in the manifesto had no lasting significance for him, and in no way influenced his later practice. You do a lot of things when you are young!

For my own part, my attitude to sound was at that time exactly the same as it is today. Suppose I am talking. I film the scene and record the sound. If you show it on the screen you will see my action and the words that accompany it. That is the unity. It is speech which distinguishes us from the lower animals. Our great biologist Pavlov said that speech makes us human beings. That is exactly my view.

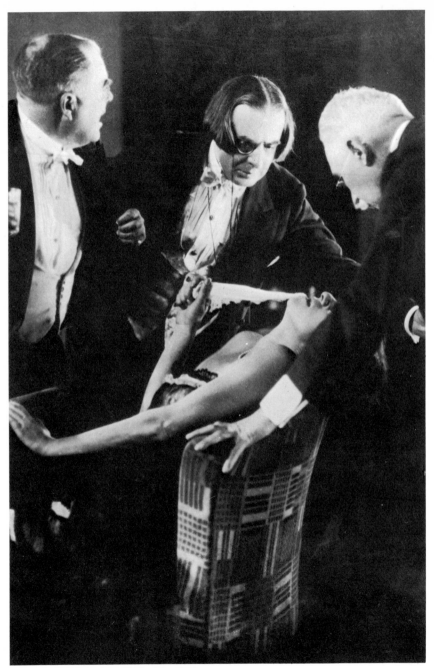

The End of St Petersburg (Pudovkin, 1927)

A talking actor is a thousand times more expressive than a silent actor (although in certain circumstances a gesture can be more expressive than a word). Sound is part of the actor's means. Hence I have always defended sound. I was incidentally one of the first to bring information about sound systems to the Soviet Union. I had gone to Germany with Pudovkin, and was one of the first Soviet film-makers to study the Tri-Ergon sound system. I talked with its inventors and as I had a certain technical ability, I was able to grasp the process. On my return I passed the information on to my colleagues. That, I think, was in 1928.

On the question of the impression that films like *Potemkin* and *Mother* made when they were first shown, I can best recall a phrase by Béla Balázs which I used as epigraph to my first course at VGIK: 'We first learned to express feelings visually, and to make them understood.' The form of films like *Potemkin* and *Mother* was new, and surprised the audience, demanding a certain participation from them. Today you can show any kind of montage and everyone will understand it. At that time it was much more complicated. We watched the reactions of audiences very carefully, going round all the cinemas in which *Mother* was shown. And it got across! I am speaking now of the montage of the scenes acted by the actors. Everything that the actor expressed: say a smile, a look, a gesture – it was all put over on the screen with complete clarity. The montage was logical and clear. And it worked because of that. Pudovkin's aim was to express the psychological states of the characters through the montage.

It must be remembered that mime and action, filmed in general long shots, had been a complete failure. Zheliabuzhski's *Polikushka*, with Moskvin, was really not a success, even though the actor was brilliant. The playing did not get across.

Pudovkin studied all this, and montage enabled him to avoid useless gesturing on the part of the actors, enabled him to concentrate the attention of the spectators. And we always had felt that films like *Mother*, and more particularly *The End of St Petersburg*, were perfectly understood by audiences.

Especially when they had a good musical accompaniment. Remember that at that time special scores were written for important films, and in the best cinemas they were always shown with their proper musical accompaniment. So for *The End of St Petersburg* several musical phrases evoked immediate and very precise associations. For example, in the scene of the patriotic demonstration the music played a slightly distorted version of the national anthem – the two perceptions, visual and aural, were linked and mutually reinforced. Pudovkin's films never baffled their audiences.

Potemkin, too, was always very clear and precise, despite the elaborations and the complexity of the montage; for it was again a case of a *narrative* montage and not an *associational* montage

But when you come to associational montage. . . . Spectators were used to seeing realities on the screen and not associations, not the ulterior significance

Mother

of things. That was another affair. In *October* the associations did not get across. When they saw Kerensky and then a balalaika, people did not understand it. They said, 'Yes, that is Kerensky, but what's a balalaika doing in it?' Later, perhaps, when they got home, a few would understand: 'Ah, yes, Kerensky bla-blas like a balalaika!'

Some things are in the very nature of cinema. We understood this, and for us only the setting could create the atmosphere of a film. We used the landscape in *Mother* because we were convinced that it could express not only the landscape as a place, but, further, the interior tonality of the moment, the ambience. In *Mother* there is a montage of springtime: the sparkle of the sun on the water, the melting snow. Everybody derived from this a very clear, very precise association – rebirth. Pudovkin had discovered associations which were entirely acceptable and accepted by everyone. They had to be sufficiently simple and natural to be immediately understood. When the washbowl ran over in the scene of the father's death, all the audience understood: the silence was such that you seemed to hear the water splashing.

Pudovkin could find the simplest methods and the only ones that got across; because complicated methods do not achieve their end. He discovered them without knowing in advance how he was going to work. Critics know, maybe; but we film-makers learn empirically, by experience, by success and failure.

Mother

What is a theory? It is experience codified. I learned theory when we were making the Pavlov film. Do you know how Pavlov created a theory? By thousands of experiments, minutely controlled and studied. Then he deduced a law from his results. How many dogs were sacrificed! Simply to arrive at a precise conclusion. That is why we, too, got into the habit of basing everything on experience.

Now I teach my profession to the young. Have I the right to tell them things which are not verified, something vague, and which cannot give precisely ascertained results?

I have still less right to tell a young man what he must do. I can tell him what he ought to think; but what his thoughts *will* be depends only on himself. If he has talent his thoughts will be interesting; and there will be in them something else besides memories of what he has heard at school.

We give him a method, the way to work. Let us take a very simple example: you have to make a cupboard. You can proceed like this: here is an existing cupboard which appears to be made of wood; so perhaps it is necessary to take a tree and cut it up? But if you have been taught by a good method, you are going to proceed thus: first, determine what the cupboard is for; then determine its dimensions; then study the most appropriate material for its construction; then draw the plans, look for the best methods of manufacture, and so on. In other words, we teach our students the best methods of work to obtain the most perfect result.

When we talk about teaching a young man to make films, it means that we first of all teach him – if he is a director – not to write scripts. Secondly, if you are the director of a film adapted from a literary work – respect its author. Then he is taught: you are going to make a film, let us say, on the life of engineers. What do you know about their lives? Nothing? Then learn about it. When you have learnt, when you know this living material, only then can you begin to prepare your film.

We teach him also that every work must have a social value; that he does not create it for his personal amusement, but for people; that he has no right to create works that are harmful to society. For instance we are often asked: why don't we show a film like *The Seven Samurai* in the Soviet Union? Simply because if we did, louts would begin to fight with knives.

In short, the method is a series of 'hows' – how to study the material, how to treat it, what aims to set, how to organize the work. All this is learned by practice of the craft.

As to the work of the cameraman, you must remember the words of Stanislavsky: 'To play this scene, you have to place an arm-chair. How to place it? Ah, for that you already need talent.'. In principle I never blame young cameramen for getting carried away by the possibilities – often acrobatic – that the camera offers. If the man is intelligent, after being excessively carried away, he will be better able to try something really good and really useful. We do not think that it is useful to forbid anything in this field. Of course, there are those who make mistakes . . . one can only hope that the mistakes will disappear in the next film. The best thing would be if all the mistakes were committed in the course of the years of study, but unhappily it is not always the case.

But you cannot forbid experiment. No one knows in advance whence something good may emerge. The critics know maybe; but we don't.

Let us take an example: *Shadows of Our Forgotten Ancestors*. That is a film made in a very interesting way, but full of errors. For a start it is too long. Much too long. Then it is far from being intelligible to everyone. For me it is interesting, because I understand Ukrainian, I know this particular ethnography, these popular songs, these yule-tides, these rituals. I am equally interested by the way of showing all this – a purely poetic way. But for many people all this remains incomprehensible. This film is not designed for what is called the average audience. But why be hard on the authors on that account? It is useful. They will do better next time.

We always seek new things. If people only look back on their own histories – mine among others . . . God Almighty! But I could write volumes about experiments made by Pudovkin and myself which went straight into the bin without anyone ever seeing them. We saw for ourselves that we were making mistakes. But if someone doesn't realize when he has embarked on something that is not to be done – that is irremediable!

There are arts in which it is possible to create works of value by possessing only talent, and not intelligence. A cinema director must have both talent and intelligence. That is why you do not often meet directors of outstanding value. The job demands too much.

Why do I think that a director ought not to write scenarios? Again, no one forbids people to do anything. But what happens in practice? Generally the most complex things are considered the most simple. Everyone thinks he can write a novel. Why? Because no one can teach you *how* to write good novels. For my own part I think it is better for directors not to write scenarios. My argument is quite simple: to write a novel like, for instance, *Quiet Flows the Don*, you need to know absolutely and to feel deeply the life of the Don Cossacks. And who, I would like to know, can penetrate to the heart of a matter in this way if he has to go each day to the studios and never meets anyone but assistants, editors and so on? Dovzhenko wrote his scenarios, certainly. But when Dovzhenko wrote *Earth* (which in my opinion is his greatest film) he knew what he was talking about. He was of the earth himself. . . . And when he wrote *Poem of the Sea*, he lived a year in New Khakhovka, among the dam-builders and the kolkhoz people. How many writer-directors can one name? Chaplin, Dovzhenko – and who else?

Pudovkin did not write his scenarios. And Eisenstein did not want to write his. There are people who can do everything. We had Lomonosov who was at once chemist, physician and poet. Today at Moscow University the students are divided into 'modern subjects' and 'arts'. They say that they are incompatible things, that a physicist cannot write poems. But Lomonosov wrote them.

The Feast of Tzai in *Storm Over Asia* (Pudovkin, 1928)

Pudovkin never interfered with the dramaturgy of a script. He had had one experience of it – the trial scene from *Mother*. A very significant example. Preparing the cutting script, Pudovkin was so taken up with this scene that to realize it as he had written it would have made a whole film – that scene alone would have been more than 1,500 metres. So he asked Zarkhi, 'Nathan, disentangle it: extract what is necessary for the dramaturgy of the film.' It was perfectly natural: the director gets carried away by his work and loses sight of the total composition of the film, which the writer keeps always in his mind.

In the case of scripts, my own role in the work with Pudovkin and Zarkhi was purely consultative. The prison scene in *Mother*, for instance. Neither Pudovkin nor Zarkhi had ever been in prison. But I had three times had a taste of it in the German occupation, as I had been a partisan. That was in 1918, and I still remembered pretty well what prison is like. And I told them. For *The End of St Petersburg* I was, to some extent, the author of the idea for the film.

The idea of making *Storm Over Asia* from the Novokchonov novel was originally suggested to Pudovkin, if I remember rightly, by Aleinikov. Pudovkin accepted, as he put it, 'only for Golovnya'. The fact is that the book was not at all in the style of the films he normally made. Pudovkin at that time was extremely tired, literally exhausted. Nowadays it is hard to imagine just

The Feast of Tzai in *Storm Over Asia*

what it was like to live in Moscow between 1920 and 1927. Seven years of uninterrupted work, living under extremely difficult conditions and in constant nervous tension. Pudovkin undertook to do the film as a kind of holiday, since it was to be shot far away from the strained atmospheres of the studios.

Zarkhi was initially asked to do the scenario, but he refused. Then Osip Maximovitch Brik was offered it. A friend of Mayakovski, he was a highly intelligent man and a fine writer. Within a week he had made a scenario out of the novel – nineteen typed pages, in which each scene was described in at most four words. In other words, a real silent film scenario, in the old, admirable way of montage scenarios.

I went off to the Bouriato-Mongolian Republic, in March 1928. I went ahead – to look for locations and get everything ready for Pudovkin. What I found there proved to be very interesting. When Pudovkin arrived we took a car and toured the locations; and Pudovkin was very pleased with them.

We had been given an adviser: Achirov, a Bouriato-Mongol and an extremely cultured man who knew perfectly Chinese, Mongolian, Russian, and, I believe, French. In general the Mongols are extremely intelligent. In conversations with Pudovkin, Achirov proved able to give living flesh to our skeleton scenario. I found these discussions absolutely thrilling. Achirov told us about the life of his countrymen, their customs, their way of life. And so, without changing anything in the scenario itself – for Pudovkin never altered scenarios – we began our work, basing it on Achirov's stories and on the living ethnographical material.

Take for instance the Feast of Tzai, which did not exist in the original scenario any more than the other scenes which resulted from our contacts with the actual life of the monasteries, which still existed there at that time and made a great impression upon us. Just imagine: in steppe-land, absolutely flat and swept by violent winds, there were those temples with their unique turned-up roofs, with silver bells suspended at each corner. You would be driving along the steppe and hear, coming from nowhere, a silvery chime. It was very surprising.

There was a lake there, overrun with game. The lamas and the Mongolians in general were then not allowed to hunt, nor to work the fields. It was regarded as a terrible sin. It is not so long ago since they abandoned this belief. If you walked beside this lake in European clothes, all the birds would fly away. But if you dressed as a lama, they wouldn't budge – just like the pigeons in St Mark's Square.

They were very interesting people, and very courteous. For instance, the Feast of Tzai is always celebrated on a certain date. At Achirov's request, the Bog Do lama, the principal of the monastery, agreed to bring forward the date of the festival specially so that we could film it. But the performance of the ceremony could not be modified: the ritual had to be strictly followed, independently of the requirements of the filming. They paid absolutely no attention to us and of course there could be no retakes. I was just shown the plan of the ceremony in advance – what people would dance, when, where, and so on.

Unhappily at that time there were no hand cameras. In order to shoot all this I had a harness which held the camera on my chest. It was an old Debrie; and the motor gave up the ghost at once; so I had to operate it manually, turning the handle and all the time running right and left. Five thousand metres of film.

Generally speaking the character of the local people helped us a lot. They are very sensible. Nothing surprises them; they continued about their business without paying any attention to the camera. They did all the market scenes themselves, at our request, perfectly calmly and amiably and exactly as we wanted. They are really excellent people.

When we needed to collect a large number of them together for the final scenes, the aeroplane served as bait. We offered them trips in the plane. Well, as I say, nothing surprised them! They saw an aeroplane for the first time in their lives, and they got into it as calmly as might be – a man must not show that he is frightened of anything. As for the monks, the lamas, it was even more simple: they said that all this had already existed long ago, only men had not considered it useful, so had forgotten it. . . .

Pudovkin was very impressed by all this. We made the film, with a very strong feeling for all its living material.

The final scenes of the storm were created out of the nature of the place itself. We Europeans find it hard to realize the enormous scale of this landscape. There a river is a vast river and a mountain is a real mountain, soaring right up to the heavens. Everything is immense – trees, men, everything.

While we were shooting we did not know what was going to come of it. We only knew that afterwards. The triumph was when the film was shown in Germany. Pudovkin went off to be present at each evening's presentation, and he came back from them literally covered with laurels. The Japanese also regard the film as the basis of all cinematography. And if I were asked which of my films I prefer, I would place *Storm Over Asia* immediately after *Mother*.

In conclusion: as a teacher I am very attentive to the methods used in training sports teams, especially footballers. Because in no other field is the method of training so evidently linked to the results obtained, and to the possibility of deeply exploring the personality of a man in all its aspects.

Experience shows that a good runner needs not only strong legs, but also an intelligent brain to discover the best tactics for a race. A good footballer is not necessarily the fastest runner, but the one who thinks best. An instance: I have to train a cameraman. To give him the sense of light, the sense of form. What am I going to do? I learn from the methods of sports trainers, those who form world champions.

Let us put it more simply. I believe that the highest form of art is the circus. When a man can walk on a tightrope – he can walk. When he can not, he breaks his head. And all that is very *visible*. In the circus you *have* to work. While in the cinema. . . .   (Recorded in Moscow, July 1965)

Alexander Dovzhenko

10. Alexander Petrovitch Dovzhenko

History brings constant revaluations, but two reputations in the Soviet cinema are unassailable: Eisenstein and Dovzhenko. Dovzhenko was born in September 1894, the child of Ukrainian peasants. He was a late starter in the Soviet cinema at a time when most of its leaders had taken up film direction in their late teens and early twenties. He had been a teacher, then a diplomat attached to the consulates in Warsaw and Berlin. Then he had taken up painting and been cartoonist for a Kharkov newspaper. In 1926, aged thirty-two, he read in one of the avant-garde journals of the time that painting was the art of the past. Persuaded, he impulsively packed his bag and went to the Odessa film studios.

Oddly, in view of the lyrical and passionate and patriotic vision of the later days, he wanted to be a director of comedy, and to the end of his life prided himself on his physical resemblance to Chaplin. His first film was a two-reel comedy nearer in style to Max Linder than to Keystone, *The Little Fruits of Love*. His characteristic visual style is more evident in his first full-length film, *The Diplomatic Pouch*, a rip-roaring adventure story about two Soviet couriers carrying important documents who are waylaid and murdered by the British secret police. Only the solidarity of the honest British sailor lads, led by Bo'sun Harry, saves the documents and the day.

Dovzhenko's uniqueness was only revealed for the first time with *Zvenigora* (1928), a wild and wonderful affair which took a lot of explaining away to the bosses at VUFKU, the Ukrainian film organization. Eisenstein has described how the puzzled officials brought the picture to him as the most respected figure in the industry, and how he and Pudovkin sat enthralled through this lyrical fantasy which spreads over a thousand years of time, with the same group of characters recurring through the ages and with wizard-monks who emerge from the earth, horses that are painted in strange colours and a man who advertises his suicide as a theatrical entertainment, but then makes off with the takings. Next came *Arsenal* (1929), a film about the revolutionary struggles of 1918 – his most intense and concentrated work, a fiery assembly of every kind of element of caricature, folklore, drama, all welded into a single lyrical vision.

Earth (1930) remains his masterpiece. It is a story of small banal happenings; an old man dies; a collective buys a tractor; the young farm chairman is shot by a resentful kulak and is buried. Dovzhenko imbues these events with what Johnson called 'the grandeur of generality'. The editing of the images generates its own energy and inevitability; the poetic effects of the juxtapositions, the drama, the moods, the characters combine in one staggering effect. The film opens with a death; but it must be the jolliest death in any film: old Grandfather having set himself to die joshes amiably with his old friends, munches an apple and peacefully lies down on the earth calmly watched by the village children, surrounded by a cheerful sea of fallen apples.

After *Earth* came *Ivan* in which Dovzhenko characteristically discovers lyrical exhilaration in so improbably concrete a theme as the Dnieper hydro-electric project. Montages of the construction work have a powerful sensuous effect; and the characters of the workers – even the slacker played by Stepan Shkurat – are warmer and more genial even than in Dovzhenko's other films. This is in sharp contrast to *Aerograd*, a brilliant and singularly disturbing film, reflecting so truthfully as it does the times in which it was made (1935) in its treatment of the idea that even the best friend who is an enemy of the State must be ruthlessly sacrificed. It is all the more chilling since Dovzhenko's genius is no less persuasive than in his earlier, more human films.

Stalin himself suggested the theme of *Shchors*, about the Ukrainian revolutionary hero; and his continuing interest resulted in a prolonged and uneasy production period. The film emerged, moreover, at a time of especial political difficulty. Despite these circumstances, Dovzhenko managed to give some life to the characters and the period, perhaps because of the element of autobiography.

After this it is not quite clear just what personal difficulties Dovzhenko experienced. He ceased to be head of the Kiev studios, and indeed never returned to the Ukraine after the war. His attention was diverted to war service and to writing. Films which were clearly his carried the credits of other directors. At least one of these, *Battle for the Ukraine*, made in 1944 and credited to his wife, Julia Solntseva, with Dovzhenko acknowledged only as supervisor and scenarist, now appears incontestably as part of the canon of the director's great works. The material was shot by twenty-four cameramen at various parts of the front. Although they were not directly supervised by Dovzhenko, it is said that he gave each of them detailed instructions and even drawings to show what visual effects he wanted. The film they brought back, actual reportage of death and destruction and survival of the Ukrainian land, was assembled by Dovzhenko into the last true Dovzhenko film, perhaps in some ways the most exciting of all. The images roar along, each sweeping in the next with the inevitability of a musical structure. Thrillingly these factual, often harrowing images refer back to the fiction films: the struggling horses from *Arsenal*, a dead soldier whose comrades mourn him like the peasants in *Earth*. People, like the earth and its fruits tend to survive. Alongside the war and its devastations, the peasants still work the land and the corn still grows.

After his last film, *Michurin*, and Dovzhenko's death while preparing *Poem of the Sea*, his widow loyally, heroically and bizarrely determined that his genius should not die. She completed *Poem of the Sea* then made a new 'Dovzhenko' film from one of his unrealized scripts, *Story of the Years of Flame*. The film was a success with the public and enabled Julia Solntseva to make further Dovzhenko projects. Dovzhenko's was a talent that could not, ultimately, outlive him; but the will of his widow to perpetuate this artist who perhaps suffered more than we can know in his lifetime from incomprehension and official obstruction is a touching and brave tribute to Dovzhenko's own conviction of life's continuity.

Beginnings – Sources

Beginnings

In June 1926 I left for Odessa where I began to work in the studios as a director. Thus, in my thirty-third year I was to start my life afresh, to take on a new apprenticeship: until then I had never been an actor, nor a theatrical *metteur en scène*; I went little to the cinema, had nothing to do with artists and had no knowledge of the theory or the infinite complexity of the synthetic art of the cinema. Moreover, at Odessa there was no time to learn, and perhaps there was no one who could have taught me. The cinema factory was quite important, but the cultural level was rather low and the films did not shine for any outstanding quality.

An insignificant circumstance helped me at the start. I was often present at the location shooting of an Odessa director. What he was doing with his actors was so bad, so obviously feeble, that it encouraged me. I said to myself: I see that it is bad and I know exactly what is bad and why it is bad. So I am not so completely unprovided as it seems. Indeed, I have only to do it myself and I will do it better.

This deduction was not entirely justified. How often since have I seen young people, sparkling with apparent gifts, able to analyse in detail every sequence and every shot that someone else does, and yet who appear pitiably helpless when they get the chance to direct themselves. I must say that that has never happened to me though I find the work very difficult. I've been a director for sixteen years,* yet even so, at the start of each film I feel that I know absolutely nothing. I have never been a shirker in my art, but apprehension at starting work, and constant worry remain with me and will not leave me as long as I live. The work is as multiform and limitless as is life in our great socialist society in its victorious development. And no genius, no talent can ever achieve anything in art without the support of knowledge and experience. Not only the knowledge of the specific nature of his art, but primarily and essentially, knowledge of life. The cinema demands enormous and dedicated work – not only during the making of the film, but in the mental process of its conception. The cinema is an art of possessed people.

Coming to the cinema, I thought of devoting myself entirely to comedies and comic films. My first script, *Vasya the Reformer*, was conceived as a comedy, and my first attempt at direction, *Little Fruits of Love*, belonged to the same genre. Likewise my unrealized films are all conceived as comedies: *Homeland*, about the Jews in Palestine, *Chaplin Lost*, about the life of Chaplin on a desert island, and *Tsar*, a satirical comedy about the life of Nicholas II. But things turned out differently and I only made a single comedy. I've always taken a lot of pleasure in the few comic passages which have been scattered through my films. The comedy that we do in the Soviet cinema always seems to me for some reason feeble and false in principle. I do not know why, but we always deprive comic characters of intelligence when one must in fact do exactly the opposite. A comic character is not one with a frustrated or embryonic intelligence.

Scenarists, Directors, Actors

Often the writer who comes to the cinema has not yet sufficient respect for our art to abandon to it all the power and the passion of his talent. Some writers do not understand that the world of cinematographic images is a unique and enchanted world. You cannot gallop across it on your literary charger just like that. The horse must become a cinema horse. Because of this a lot of directors, especially young ones, find themselves in an impasse, faced with a bulky book of mysteries entitled 'Literary scenario'. It was possible to *write* such a scenario, but to realize it on the screen is impossible. First it has to be translated from the 'literary'. Then of course, if the director is young, not too clever, and into the bargain too sure of himself, it's a foregone conclusion that he is going to come to grief. . . .

The scenarist must write a script that is really visual, and even give indications for the future director specifying that such a passage must be realized like this and not otherwise. Because it can happen that directors given a script can make a film totally different from that of the scenario. 'Well, I read it like that,' they say. There are different sorts of freedom of interpretation. The freedom of a subjective reading. . . . It is not that this

---

* Written in 1942.

freedom must be crushed, but that it must be limited by the liberty of the writer who also claims his freedom and who, as the primary author of the work, has an undeniable right.

[In our plays and our films] all the characters explain to one another in the same oversimplified fashion what they are going to do next. Practically nothing in context. All on one and the same level. Total absence of thought process. The absence of context in the roles deprives the actors of the possibility of creating living characters. They do not live; that is to say they do not think ('I think, therefore I am'). They are speakers of dialogue.

To bring feeling to the stage or to the screen is not difficult. It is difficult to present *thought*. What is life, if not a continual process, infinitely complex, of the conflict of impulses, ideas, individual and mass thoughts? And what can actors do if they do not think, because they have not been taught to think? Because of this they are reciters of words, or rather actors who *act* thought without thinking.

Zvenigora

What can there be more unacceptable in a film than the title: 'Twenty years have passed . . .'? Right up to the present, unity of time rules in the cinema as two-dimensional representation reigned for centuries in Egyptian art.

The chiaroscuro which gives three dimensions to painting and which seems to us so comprehensible and legitimate had to fight for centuries for acceptance. It was opposed and attacked as madness or magic. In the domain of cinematic unity of time, the tenacity of certain directors and writers, slaves to conservative inertia, really reaches a peak of virtuosity. A film with three or four actors, a film in which all the action takes place in one room and almost a single day – that's the latest fashion.

What are audiences going to say when they see presented before them, in six reels of film, a thousand years? And, into the bargain, without any 'story', without passion, without Asta Nielsen? . . .

The Sources

I used to love to sleep on top of the full hay-cart and I loved to be carried into the house, heavy with sleep, when the cart stopped in the yard in front of our cottage. I loved the squeak of the wheels of the laden wagon at harvest time. I loved the twittering of the birds in the garden and in the fields, I loved the gentle croaking of the toads in the marshes in the spring, when the waters fell. I loved it when the apples fell in the meadow, in the evening, in the twilight – quite unexpected, rather secretly, they fell on the earth, in the grass. There was a mystery, something eternally unfathomable in that falling of fruit.

But more than anything else in the world I loved music. If I were asked what music, what instrument, what musicians I loved in my first childhood, I would reply that most of all I loved to hear the beating of a scythe. When, some calm evening round about the feast of Peter and Paul, my father began

Zvenigora (Dovzhenko, 1928)

Earth (Dovzhenko, 1930) and *Ivan* (Dovzhenko, 1932)

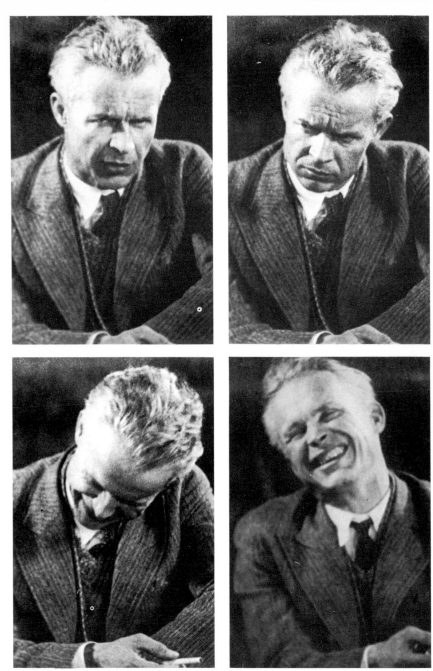

Alexander Dovzhenko

to use the scythe in the meadow, near to the house, it was the most exquisite of all music for me. I loved it so much, I waited for it as, perhaps, only the angels awaited the Easter bells – forgive me the comparison, Lord! . . . Still today it sometimes seems to me that if someone started to use a scythe under my window, I would at once become younger, kinder, better; and I would fling myself into work. From my earliest years the high, pure sound of the scythe spoke to me of joy and pleasure.

Even today, when I close my eyes, I do not know darkness. Now, still, my brain lights up with a vivid and continual glow the visible and the invisible procession of images – innumerable, sometimes without pattern. The images float over the Danube and over the Desna. The clouds in the sky float free and capriciously; they swim in the vast blue emptiness and meet in so many combats and duels that if I could only snatch a tiny part to put it into books or into films, I would not have lived on this earth in vain and I would not in vain have given annoyance to my superiors.

11. Yevgeni Iosipovitch Gabrilovitch

Gabrilovitch's charming and wryly entertaining autobiographical reminiscences hint at the hazards of artistic work under bureaucracy; and touch frankly on some weaknesses of Soviet film-making. He was born on 29 September 1899 and began his career as a writer in 1921. He entered the cinema at the end of the 1920s as 'consultant' on scientific, documentary and propaganda films. His first film credit was for the sub-titles of a late silent film, B. Chelontsev's *Harry Goes into Politics* (1933). As a film theorist he upholds the theory of a 'cine-prose', the importance of the scenario as a literary genre in its own right. Principal films from his scenarios: *The Last Night* (Yuli Raizman, 1937; from Gabrilovitch's novel *Gentle Brovkin*), *Mashenka* (Raizman, 1942), *The Dream* (Mikhail Romm, 1943), *Two Combatants* (Leonid Lukov, 1943), *Matriculate 217* (Romm, 1945), *In the Name of Life* (Heifetz and Zarkhi, 1947), *Our Heart* (Alexander Stolper, 1947), *Harvest* (Pudovkin, 1955), *Sunrise over the Niemen* (Alexander Faintzimmer, 1953), *The Gadfly* (Alexander Faintzimmer, 1955), *The Lesson of Life* (Raizman, 1955), *Two Captains* (Vladimir Vengerov, 1956), *Murder in Dante Street* (Romm, 1956), *The Communist* (Raizman, 1958), *Stories About Lenin* (Yutkevitch, 1958), *Resurrection* (Mikhail Schweizer, 1960–2), *The Difficult Hour* (I. Gurin, 1961), *Lenin in Poland* (Yutkevitch, 1966).

Adventures and Encounters of a Scenarist

All my life, especially in my youth, I have hated mathematics. But I always loved to dream that like Einstein I would produce the solution to some quite unimaginable problem in two brilliant pages. I would become famous, and the maths teacher of the gymnasium (that is where the dream became especially voluptuous!), would cry out, dazzled by my glory: 'Oh, how blind I have been!' I wanted more than anything to be a writer. I did not like writing any more than I liked solving equations, but I liked to dream that I had become a writer, that all the newspapers talked about me, that my novels and stories were thrilling, that my life would flower so splendidly that even my father (who hated writers) would exclaim, his hands thrown up to heaven: 'Lord, how wrong I was!'

But all that was only dreams, and my father wanted me to become an engineer. So, when I left the gymnasium I presented myself for the entrance examination at the Moscow Technical High School. That was in 1919, in a country that had been disorganized and devastated by the Civil War. The disorganization had reached the school likewise. Water streamed through the ceilings – as it did through most ceilings in those times. In the big hall, which hadn't been swept for ages, bits of yellowed paper, maybe left over from last year's examinations, blew about. The wind which came through the broken windows wrapped the scraps of paper about the feet of the professor. The

Yevgeni Gabrilovitch

candidates kept on their coats, and so did the examiner, despite the relative warmth of the autumn temperature. His method of testing our knowledge was to give each candidate a different question: I was gratified to receive one which I was totally incapable of solving. Thinking it over, I decided I preferred to exchange it with my neighbour's, the more so since he had already solved his. But the supervisor who had seemed so stupid all wrapped up as he was, caught me at once and threw me out of the examination room. I tried pleading, but he was as ice. It does not take much imagination to picture the tears and reproaches which greeted my return under the parental roof.

So bang went my dreams of becoming Einstein, Maxwell or Lobachevski. I became a worker in a saccharine factory. At that time aristocrats and bourgeois sold not only their overcoats and jackets, but also their libraries. In the market, alongside the oatmeal and plum marmalade (sold clandestinely) books were sold in bulk. One day I bought *The History of Economic Science*, and after reading it I discovered that my vocation was to be an economist. I wanted to become a new Marx, a new Proudhon, a new Adam Smith. Preferably Proudhon, though, because his life seemed more dramatic than the others.

As I have said, I was working in the saccharine factory. But because of shortages of raw materials, we turned over to making glaziers' putty. When the stocks of linseed oil gave out, the factory definitively stopped work and I was able to devote myself more actively to political economy. I wrote an article on Proudhon without having read a line of his works, simply using my *History*, my bedside book. A little later I noticed on the bookstalls a little magazine called *Life*, which appeared twice a month and which happened – choosing its words with great care, naturally – to express certain points of disagreement with the doctrine of Marx himself. I told myself that what was needed was my article on Proudhon and I went to see the publishers. It was a modest office, a room in a communal apartment, with a folding bed along one wall, a sack of potatoes in a corner and a pile of books in another. The editor, fair-haired and about twenty-six, wearing the jacket of a PTT employee over a bright red Russian shirt, welcomed me joyfully: he published the magazine single-handed and at his own expense, and a well-wishing collaborator was more precious to him than a brother. He read my article and said it would not do – a lot had already been published on Proudhon. However my talent as a journalist was evident and he commissioned me to write an article on the theme 'Love and Friendship'.

Around five months later, I stumbled upon an announcement which invited citizens of both sexes and all ages to present themselves in Jitnaia Street, in order to take part in the crowd scenes of a film on the Revolution. I was young, and full of vague hopes; and I dreamed of trying my powers in the cinema. Early one winter morning, in the mist and the snow, I reported to Jitnaia Street. Our faces were covered in a thick layer of grease and we were told that we were to represent a group of peasants who were watching a kulak's house burning. There was no fire, of course, but we were told to imagine that we saw one. Then it was that I saw for the first time in my life, a film director. He was wearing a cap, breeches and a check jacket, and he kept on tearing at his hair. In the way he moved and yelled through the megaphone there was such a transport of wild will, such pathetic devotion to the cause of beauty that, watching him, dumb with admiration, I quite forgot the imaginary fire. Till then I had never seen with what abnegation directors will tear their hair when art is involved.

Notwithstanding the mègaphone, only three scenes were shot that morning, after which the extras, stupefied by the make-up and the lights, were permitted a rest. At once everybody untied the bits of rag which wrapped their lunches in this time of military communism. And then it came out that these down-at-heel bearded men had not so long ago been habitués of grand mansions in the fashionable quarters of the town, and of the English Club. Munching their black bread, they recalled the balls of the old days, even the coronation of Nicholas II, though this they mentioned only in lowered voices and with cautious glances, because the director's assistants were everywhere.

Then the lights went on again, the flurry was resumed, the director's voice thundered orders, something was hoisted up with great cries, and a man who wore his cap back to front started to turn the handle of the magic machine.

165

And all this was so astonishing, overwhelming, stupefying, miraculous, and I was so captivated by this process of artistic, cinematographic creation at which I was present for the first time, that I quite forgot my role. Suddenly I heard the director howling, fixing me with a furious stare: 'Hey! Yes, you down there! What the hell do you think you're mucking about at?' But even this cry seemed to me astonishing and marvellous, because it was the first time in my life that I had been addressed by a film director. Since that time many film directors have addressed equally unfriendly words to me, but that has not stifled my passion for the art of the cinema. I believe even that it was at that very moment, at that very spot in Jitnaia Street that this indestructible love was born. However often I try to escape from it by devoting mysel' to other occupations, it still takes possession of me again with a still more ardent flame. And that is how, that memorable winter, I fell by chance on an announcement that changed my life – for better or worse.

It is more than thirty years ago now that I was mobilized into the art of the cinema. One of the first appeals was put out, asking writers to come to work in the cinema. So there I was in an office, facing one of the directors of the State Cinema Committee and listening to a speech on the crucial role of the writer who decides to devote himself to films. The director was young, ardent and had lots of hair. He was an experienced orator and the prospects of my creative flowering (if I agreed to become a scenarist) were revealed to be so brilliant that to refuse would have been simply foolish. Thus it was that I became scenarist-editor of cultural films and propaganda agit-films – genres which were then considered the most important for our cinema.

The 'Culturefilm' Studio was in a strange part of town: tortuous, sinister corridors led to anonymous offices, in which the tables of script editors vanished under heaps of annotated and corrected scenarios. The studio not only made cultural and political propaganda films, but also slogans and posters. The editors (also known as 'consultants') had the task of watching over the artistic level of the scenarios and hunting out political errors – they were found in mass-production quantities. Every day there were several meetings to discuss scenarios, which were required to answer to a collection of demands of granite rigorousness. The 'consultants' watched over what was 'reflected': the development of the mechanism, the new techniques, the preponderant role of social organizations and so on. To be fair, however, I must say that it was enough to introduce into a propaganda scenario a close-up of a door with the inscription 'Syndical Section' and to show a shock worker entering this door in order for it to be considered proved (in artistic terms) that the worker in question was included in and guided by the Syndicate. And when an author had not the possibility to talk in detail about new techniques, it was enough to show the shock workers poring over the blueprints of new machines.

Generally the scenarios were discussed long and minutely. Then the reports were drafted. The authors brought their corrections, new reports were written and so on. But I realized quite quickly that this had no real importance, because the director and his cameraman, once on location, made their film not according to the scenario but according to their own inspiration and the chances for improvisation presented during shooting. Almost invariably the filming was pure improvisation, and all the corrections, the discussions about the corrections, the corrections of the corrections and the new discussions which followed – all this became, on the spot, pointless. Bronzed and cheery, the director and the cameraman brought back from their expedition quite unforeseen material – unforeseen not merely by the 'consultants' but no doubt also by themselves. Then it all began again. A new scenario was written in relation to what had been shot, the new titles were drafted and, often, the cultural film in course of being made was transformed into a propaganda or popular instructional film, even reportage. This was called 'salvaging the material'. I quickly realized that the essential work of a consultant was to discover an effective method of mitigating the chronic deficiencies of the material filmed. Among the consultants there were brilliant specialists in this kind of salvage work, but sometimes even these men admitted their powerlessness. Then a consultation would be arranged with outside people – this was the council of the magi. The most famous of them was Victor Shklovski. His solutions, the titles which he suggested, were often real artistic discoveries and the apparently expired film was brought back to life.

I have the impression that I succeeded quite well – not merely in the editing of reports, but also in the field of salvage and re-editing of films. I soon won promotion and was transferred (with an appreciable salary increase) into the Feature Film Department. For some time my friends and my wife had been trying to persuade me to leave the cinema and go back to writing. I knew perfectly well that I had to get out of all this, that these corrections of corrections were simply a waste of time; that I must leave, fly, take up paper and pen again. But it was already too late. I could not tear myself from this work. It seemed that this art, still in its infancy, concealed strange, incomprehensible possibilities. And vague, unknown, uncertain paths offered themselves as in a dream.

When I think back on my meditations at that time, it seems to me that, despite my nascent love, I might well have said farewell to the art of the cinema. But at that moment the star of the silent cinema suddenly began to wane, despite impassioned attempts to uphold it. And rapidly and irresistibly there began to climb in the heavens the unknown and mysterious star of the sound film, alternatively known as 'cinema with noises and conversation'. I took up my new job at the Feature Film Studios at the critical moment when all around were embattled, cursing, railing and insulting the rising star to the best of their ability.

It is hard to imagine how difficult the journey to the Potylikha Studios was then.* From the Kiev Station, to the south-west, little trams threaded the

---

* Now Mosfilm Studios. Moscow has now grown to take in this formerly remote suburb.

banks óf the Moskva. Filled beyond bursting, they rattled on broken rails along a broken-up highway. The slaves of the young and joyful muse of cinematography generally preferred to make the journey on foot. From the Okrujnoi Bridge there was no proper road. We struggled up the hill by a sort of footpath and, floundering in mud, we arrived at the peculiar structure, of which the evening paper spoke so often and with such wild enthusiasm. The paper admired particularly the architectural plan of the studios: in conformity with the principles of 'agit-architecture'* the studio was built in the shape of an aeroplane!

The building was not yet finished and the stages were not equipped for sound, so that the first talking pictures were made elsewhere, on Lesnaia Street. At Potylikha there were only preparations for filming – with splendid facilities, as *Moscow Evening* was only too glad to reveal. Waiting, in unheated rooms with unplastered walls, sat the consultants, the accountants, the editors and the administrative team. In the corridors roamed the directors, in search of scenarios. I remember Okhlopkov, Pyriev, Abram Room, Medvedkin. Eisenstein was then working in Mexico and his film was spoken of with religious awe, as something prodigious. Sometimes Matcheret would whirl by pursued by his bubbling assistant Micha. They were then making *Works and Men* and Micha, a scenarist, had had the idea of serving a period as assistant cameraman. No one at Potylikha then imagined that this Micha, under the name of Mikhail Romm, would make the first feature film about Lenin.

The builders of the aeroplane-building had, among other things, succeeded in achieving a remarkable thermal effect: during the winter, an insupportable cold filled the offices, while the heat in summer made them quite uninhabitable. On the other hand in the innumerable corridors, the climate was invariably temperate. So it was there that the film-makers collected for violent discussions about the problems of artistic creation.

What subjects there were to discuss in those far-off days! How should one depict the positive hero – simply positive, or with some human flaw? May the heroine of a film be pretty, or is that a concession to bourgeois taste? What is optimism and what pessimism? In what lies decadence and in what heroism? How to vanquish formalism? How should satire be made an affirmation of life? How should one react to the evident lack of political culture of certain young masters of cinema who take themselves much too seriously? Does the worker class need fiction films or documentaries? With or without a story? With or without a personal drama? What best accentuates the heroism of the masses – everyday heroism or monumental romanticism?

But the essential question, which brought bitterness, passion, despair to these discussions, was the problem of sound films. Those who only know

---

* 'Agit-architecture' is an ironic usage based on the terms 'agit-film', 'agit-train', etc. The aeroplane-building of Mosfilm has given birth to innumerable anecdotes, even legends, like that of the 'lost office' where unhappy wanderers, lost in the maze of corridors and stairways, are ultimately stranded and are condemned to stay, vainly hoping for release. . . .

sound cinema cannot imagine the panic which struck writers, directors, actors, cameramen and editors that moment when, quite unexpectedly, the cinema screen gave forth sounds. Documents in the archives, the stenograms and articles of the period are only a pale and fleeting reflection of all the emotion, the worry, the panic. For it was all the poetry of film art, believed to be of its essence mute, that was in the balance, and threatened with extinction.

Without Dramas or Conflicts

I belong to the generation whose youth coincided with the October Revolution. And I believe (probably through excessive pride) that this Soviet generation had to follow a path marked out by events, tensions and efforts unparalleled in the world.

No doubt there have been periods of equal sacrifice. But there has been no epoch of such *grandeur*.

My generation of Soviet men achieved immense things in the sciences and technology. My generation of Soviet men achieved infinitely less in the field of the arts. The art of the screen was most evident. Certainly, there were not a few good things on the screen during those years. Talented works were not so rare. And yet, in my view, the cinema did not assume its full duty.

Let us imagine a piece of squared paper, a graph on which, year by year or month by month are noted the salient events of the forty-five years of our country's existence. Let us mark with a pin those events which have inspired cinema art – one pin for every good film. We shall obtain compact masses of pins in certain squares of the graph (for instance the Civil War and the Second World War) and a few rare points scattered over the rest of the page. Yet there is no square which does not offer material and pretext for a film of great breadth, of violent passion, of profound reflectiveness. That is the incomparable gift which the Soviet era has brought to art.

But where are these films? They are very few.

Why? Here is one cause. For long years it was considered that to be 'actual', art must reveal not the essence of the life of the people, not the truth of the moral and social tempests which accompany a gigantic and stupefying industrialization of the country, but rather should illustrate the administrative activities of the times. And moreover in such a way that in the final scenes of the film all the administrative decisions must be visibly realized and, equally visibly, all administrative activities must be demonstrated triumphant.

Generally, such a film would begin with some misfortune. Then, the administrative organization having in the nick of time exposed all its causes, everything would come right in the end. Almost all these films have disappeared without leaving any traces: my generation is the living witness of the multitude of such burials.

But there is another reason for this profusion of casualties – from the opposite point of view one might say. For long years certain film-makers devoted themselves to the real-life problems – the efforts, the difficulties, the trials and the dramas – inseparable from great accomplishments. But this cinema existed in a sort of second- or third-degree contact with reality. You could say that there existed two parallel lives: one which was actually that of the people, and which involved real human beings, fields, houses, living streets, actual joys and misfortunes; and the other, an unreal, ideal plane represented by films. It seemed that a strange game was being played, its principal rule consisting of admitting that reality is not what one actually sees and lives, but something very different, which the players take for reality and which draws them always further, always higher. And all those who played the game learned to do it without hesitation, so that their game gave a false impression of its truthfulness.

Films of this sort offended not only art, but were an affront to the heroic activity of the people which they debased, depriving it of glory by making it as light and airy as some dance step. Because the grandeur of a heroic action is inseparable from the drama of heroism: the two things are one and indivisible. And the surgeons who busy themselves in cutting up the living flesh of an art in order to cut out the drama (in its highest sense, incommensurable and overwhelming) do not raise up heroism, they efface and conceal it. This is not the removal of an appendix, but a knife to the heart.

And that is the second reason for the clear spaces on the graph of the years.

Meetings

It was in the House of the Press that I saw Eisenstein for the first time, during an evening of 'visual discussion'. Representatives of different theatres were presenting fragments from their productions on which the directors commentated with polemical discussions. Eisenstein represented Proletkult. He was still very young but seemed older than his age because he was rather short, plump and even getting a bit fat. He was saying things which at that time seemed self-evident: the old theatre is dead; Uncle Vanya and Aunt Mania have no longer a place; the masses and the Revolution do not want their jeremiads, sighs, cravats and pince-nez. What do the masses and the Revolution want from the theatre? Only (answered Eisenstein) what goes back to the sources of traditional forms of popular spectacle: circus, fairground, attractions. The new theatre must be a sort of 'montage of attractions', that is to say of shock elements which strike and dazzle.

Then I saw in the theatre a curious production by Eisenstein, *Enough Simplicity in Every Wise Man*, in which Ostrovski's characters were entirely rethought. They did tightrope balancing, whirled on trapezes and sang popular ballads of the moment. It was all amusing, but in a way cold – too salted, peppered, vinegared and mustarded, burning the eyes and confusing the ears. A lot of wit, cascades of invention and yet in the end not very gay or invigorating.

I was at the première (or one of the premières) of *Potemkin* at the little Dmitrovka cinema, and I remember the quite extraordinary storm of applause which greeted the film. I also recall a meeting at which the speakers abused to the limit of their powers the representatives of Sovkino who had failed to appreciate *Potemkin* for what it was.* Mayakovski, hurling thunderbolts, took the floor. Brusquely he went up to Eisenstein who was sitting in the middle and urged him – pointing to the Sovkino representative sitting beside him – 'Go on! Hit him!'

And I remember how Eisenstein and the Sovkino representative looked at each other, rather timid and indecisive; and how, very embarrassed, they bent their heads down and gazed at the red carpet.

A Director

I learned to play the piano from being very small and in my youth I was for a long time – around ten years – a professional pianist. I played in restaurant orchestras and the peak of my career was my period in the orchestra of the Vindava Station Restaurant, composed of eight performers. I had also a private activity – this of course was during the NEP years. At parties and weddings I played the ragtime and one-steps that were then in fashion. I played enthusiastically and recklessly and was very much in demand.

At one of these parties I met the poet Vladimir Parnakh who had come back from Paris – a very unusual thing at the time! What was even rarer was the complete ensemble of jazz instruments that he had brought back with him. I have sometimes read articles which speculate about who introduced jazz into the Soviet Union: I can guarantee that it was Parnakh (archaeologists may address themselves to me in private for further information). It was certainly Parnakh who first brought to our country a saxophone and a collection of mutes for trumpets and trombones. It was he, too, who gave the first jazz concert.

It took place in the House of the Press, the clearing-house in which all the fiercest duels on literary and artistic questions were waged, and where all the latest inventions intended to overthrow the old theatrical forms were presented. The theatre of the House of the Press, which had seen many previous demonstrations of one sort or another, was full. Parnakh delivered a scientific dissertation on jazz; there was a performance of some jazz airs – rather hit and miss since no one in Moscow could play the saxophone. When Parnakh himself executed a very bizarre dance entitled 'Totem in the form of a Giraffe' there was a storm of enthusiasm. Among those who applauded furiously and yelled for an encore was Vsevolod Emilievitch Meyerhold. He at once suggested to Parnakh the formation of a jazz orchestra for the production he was then rehearsing. Parnakh liked my way of playing the piano, in which he found a Parisian quality of relaxation. Thus it was that I entered Meyerhold's theatre, where I was to work for five years.

These five years were my theatre school. I learned the art of the theatre not in books but in the wings. In all the tumult, the feverish agitation, the enthusiasm and the mishaps of the theatre. Working sometimes as assistant director, sometimes as lighting man, sometimes as prop assistant – always

---

* After the first private screening of *Potemkin* the Sovkino report said: 'Could probably be used as a good propaganda film. Suitable for workers' clubs.'

The Last Night (Raizman, 1937)

assistant, everywhere assistant something, even assistant costumier, sewing on buttons and mending the actors' trousers. I learned the written and the unwritten laws of the stage not by cramming in books, but by going in at the deep end.

Every day I had before me an extraordinary master. I used to watch him increase tenfold the power of a scene; disguise, patch up, conceal its weaknesses. I went on tour with the actors and I got to know what they asked of the plays they were interpreting. It did not require great scholarship to know why this pleased them and that did not. It was sufficient to hear them speak their text, and to seek how the role could be improved. I was asked, by actor friends, to modify or rewrite certain parts of the text. For me it was no longer apprenticeship, but a marvellous fortune: to remove the excrescences, to put the words in their correct places; to add two phrases, to improve a line, to make the whole thing more effective, more lively. . . . Voilà! The role is transformed and the actor looks at you with a new respect. And all done out of friendship, by night, on tour in Kherson or Jitomir, in the pianist's bedroom where the drum and the trombone are also lodging.

After working for five years with Meyerhold I fell out with him and left his theatre for good – at least that is what I thought. I became a journalist, wrote a few books, then tried the peculiar and at that time scorned career of a scenarist. I wrote a scenario which became Raizman's *The Last Night*.

One summer day the telephone rang and I recognized the voice of Meyerhold, veiled with a slight huskiness: the 'Master' (as he was called in the theatre) often took cold and was troubled by hoarseness. He called me by my first name and patronymic, and maintained the formality of the second-person form of address. He said he had seen my film and wanted to have a chat with me. I will not conceal that I was struck dumb with happiness. My affection for him had remained intact despite the years, despite the violence of our misunderstanding. It was a really fervent affection, a devotion and an admiration of a force which I have never experienced for anyone else in the world of the arts.

I went to Meyerhold's home. On the walls of his apartment were *commedia dell'arte* masks, Kabuki theatre props, sketches by Golovine for *Masquerade*, photographs of Blok and Mayakovski. In the hallway – and I have never forgotten this – in the most visible place was hung a card with the telephone numbers of the fire service, ambulances, gas and electricity maintenance departments: all handy in case of emergency. All his life Meyerhold had dreads of fire, flood, escaping gas and sudden illness. Alas! Life had in store for him rather different trials.

We embraced. Then still addressing me formally, he started to say very nice things about our film. I wanted to say: No, don't! Call me by my first name, as in the past, don't speak with this emphatic politeness, but more warmly, as to your prodigal but still faithful pupil. I wanted to tell him that I loved him as before and to hell with all our quarrels; and to hell with me for having quarrelled with him! Because the man who has the chance to live alongside a unique person and who maintains recriminations and rancour is a poor mediocre thing . . . I said nothing of all this, none of these sincere and burning words – in that house their warmth and spontaneity could have seemed in doubt. And all through the months of our last acquaintance, Meyerhold continued to address me in the formal second person, and to call me Yevgeni Iosipovitch. Perhaps he did so with intentional irony – I knew only too well this side of him. . . . Whatever it was, he asked me if I was a friend of his theatre. 'A friend!' I exclaimed. Then he said that he had sworn on the grave of Nikolai Ostrovski that he would mount *And the Steel was Tempered*. And he was asking me to adapt a play from the novel.

That was really a surprise!

Meyerhold worked for a long time on a project for a monumental film about railroads. He spoke about it a great deal and with warmth. But – and this is something which I have only now understood – his researches were all very close to the cinema. He cut his plays – even classical ones – into a series of distinct episodes. For each episode he discovered a specific and complete scenic form, a determined place of action. In his hands, each episode discovered its own rhythm, an original dramaturgy in which alongside the characters created by the author there came to life other silhouettes, invented by the director – generally mute, but very active and very expressive, a kind of accompaniment to the central figure.

He used the most astonishing methods of making the spectator's viewpoint mobile, as it is in the cinema, whereas in the theatre it generally remains static and invariable. He directed his productions in such a way that the action never stuck in one place, but moved over all the width and the depth of the stage – not only in the horizontal plane but also in the vertical. The actors, for instance, would fly on a swing, or perform on a suspended walk at the height of the first or the second balcony. Thus he created what we call in the cinema the dynamic displacement of the camera angle. In Meyerhold's view the theatre of the revolutionary period was a theatre conceived for great masses of spectators, an explosive theatre without half-tones, pathetic, heroic and satirical. It was in this, precisely, that he saw the realism of the new art. He refuted charges of formalism levelled against him – in his view he was the one who was the true realist for the masses, for the future, for the Revolution. The 'theatre of the sentiments' on the contrary, was according to his (even perhaps mistaken) conviction inaccessible to the masses, hence abstract and vague.

The whole controversy centred on what should be regarded as the art of the revolutionary masses. In all fairness I think that in this debate Meyerhold completely lost the contest. Yes, the contest was lost. But the dialectic of art resides in this: Meyerhold's theatre continues to live, and still remains active in one or another of its aspects in innumerable productions – at home and among the avant-garde abroad. And it does not take any special perspicacity to see his heritage, his property, his imprint on the productions of those very directors who were later to be his most furious attackers.

What did he not dream! Meyerhold dreamed of a stage surrounded by spectators like a circus ring. Drama in the public squares, with tens of thousands of participants and audiences not only below but also above, at the windows, on the balconies, on the rooftops. For a period he regarded great mass scenes as indispensable – as a principle – in every Soviet spectacle. He worked out these scenes as a continual flow of episode-groups, so that each group as it came into the action seemed to be caught by a searchlight while the rest formed the background mass.

Can we not clearly perceive here all that would soon be used by the Soviet cinema – under different forms and in different ways? To a degree it is precisely here that one must look for the sources of *Potemkin* and the roots of the monumentalism of the Soviet cinema.

Few theatres anywhere have made so many mistakes, but few have bequeathed so many discoveries.

With the years Meyerhold's theatre underwent an apparent evolution. The Master, it seemed, began to abandon the principles of the new theatre which he had proclaimed. In place of the rough panels of wood, crudely white-washed, there appeared decorative elements, even well-painted canvases. In place of the working clothes and old shoes – coloured, elegant costumes. In place of any old objects, plain props for the action – mahogany furniture and even glasses of real crystal. The repertory underwent the same transforma-tion, became more and more removed from heroism and from the revolu-tionary satire of the early years.

This change of direction inevitably provoked protest from the former battle comrades of the Master. A crisis mounted as much in the whole area of stage practice which was associated with the name of Meyerhold as in his own theatre. I returned to the Meyerhold Theatre (with my adaptation of Ostrov-ski) at the height of this crisis. The piece was read to the actors, who compli-mented me very kindly – most of them remembered me as a jazz musician; and for a 'jazzist' the adaptation was not all that bad. Then the thing that all novice dramatists have to discover, began: there was not an actor who did not ask me to revise and above all extend his role. . . . I recopied, added and inserted new bits right up to the moment when the Master himself took the rehearsals in hand. And then everything jumped.

In the course of every rehearsal all that I had written during sleepless nights was shattered. And something quite new – unimaginable and astonish-ing – was born: this was what the Master improvised on the stage and what I would turn into a new text in the course of another sleepless night.

I remember extraordinary scenes. . . . I recall the storm of applause during the dress rehearsal, a hurricane of ovations at the end.

Some time later I opened the paper to read that the Meyerhold Theatre was closed by decision of the Committee for Artistic Affairs (which still existed then) and that, among other of the theatre's writers, I was accused of having travestied Ostrovski's novel and betrayed its author.

I decided to go to see Meyerhold and express my gratitude and my admiration for him. He embraced me, and I saw a tear in his eye. We spoke of insignificant things, about everything and nothing. I only remember that in the hallway, glancing at the card with the telephone numbers to call in the event of fire, illness or electricity failure, he turned to his wife: 'I think that this can go away, Zinotchka. I am afraid that something more serious is happening to us.'

That was the last thing I heard of him. I was never to see him again.

A Scenarist

These days everybody writes memoirs. More and more appear. I have read the recollections of doctors, singers, poets, directors, even of fat old former Muscovite merchants. But not once have I come across the memoirs of a scenarist. Has the time not arrived to fill this lacuna? To speak of those who came to the cinema at a time when the very word 'scenario' was spoken by serious writers with a disdainful half-smile? To speak of those who came to the cinema and stayed in it. Of those who have followed the whole glorious and difficult road of our cinema, fraternally sharing its victories and its defeats.

Since we have to remember, let us begin at the beginning. With the scenarist who first raised cinematographic writing to the dignity of a true literary genre. The one who, against all use and custom, was the first to regard the scenarist as a writer and the scenario as a specific form of literature.

I want to speak of Nathan Abramovitch Zarkhi, who died more than thirty years ago. Nathan Zarkhi studied at the Tver gymnasium, and then at Moscow University, in the Romano-German Languages Department. From 1920 he organized a little theatre in Rjev where he produced Verhaeren's *Dawn*. . . . Then, coming to Moscow, Zarkhi lectured on literature. And began to love cinema.

Then, all at once, he wrote a scenario. I do not know whether *The House of the Golubins* was his first work in the genre. It is possible that like the rest of us he exercised himself on scenarios that were never realized. That I do not know. But *The House of the Golubin Family* at once earned him fame. At the time there was a group of very active scenarists in Moscow. The group comprised Valentin Turkin, Georgii Grebner, Oleg Leonidov . . . and Nathan Zarkhi. They worked principally for Mejrabpomfilm. There Zarkhi met Pudovkin. The outcome was *Mother*.

What is most astonishing is that at this time, when the scenarist was a faceless man, a vague and fluid figure, *Mother* was already called 'A Film by Pudovkin and Zarkhi'. Not everyone described it like this, but I have read the phrase in contemporary reviews. So Zarkhi had won what many of us try for in vain – to be considered as author, the equal of the director.

One day Zarkhi asked me to go and see him. He was already well known, an established master in his craft of scenario-writing. He sent for me because he was seeking reinforcements for cinema dramaturgy among the young writers. I went to his home – a room in a communal apartment on Petrovsky

Boulevard. Zarkhi was small, with thin hair, and seemed more than his age. Very animated, his gestures were rapid and during our conversation he never ceased striding around the room. The room itself was quite big. A desk, two divans, books. . . . Zarkhi wore a very formal jacket and a cravat. This is what I remember about his appearance and his room.

I had come with Boris Lapin, a marvellous writer who died during the last war. There and then, without preamble, Zarkhi endeavoured to persuade us to write for the cinema (still, of course, the silent cinema). He insisted that a scenario is not a bread-and-butter job, nor a trifle tossed off by a careless pen, but that it is literature, of the true, authentic, purest blood, and that only a writer working as a writer is capable of creating a true scenario. According to him the Tolstoys and Turgenevs of modern times would, within ten years, be scenario writers. He spoke with extraordinary conviction and astonishing warmth, ceaselessly walking about with quick little steps, adjusting his tie, which was disturbed by his movement.

Everything he told us seemed eccentric in the extreme – above all the new Tolstoys and Turgenevs! But at that time everyone who talked about art expressed himself in an eccentric manner; it was considered perfectly natural. Scenarios which would replace the novel? Possible! A Turgenev of the silent cinema? Why not! Did we not see at that time the most frenzied theatrical productions competing successfully with the most illustrious established companies? It was the time of violent debates to determine where the future of Soviet theatre art lay: in the Art Theatre or in the House of the Press with its political burlesques.

But despite Zarkhi's insistence, expatiating until we were on the very doorstep about the unsuspected possibilities of scenario writing, Lapin and I did not set ourselves to writing scenarios. I asked Zarkhi how he worked with Pudovkin. He replied that he began by writing the scene alone; then Pudovkin came and corrected it; then Zarkhi would copy it all out; then Pudovkin would come back and correct again; Zarkhi recopied; then Pudovkin came. . . .

At that moment all these corrections, copyings and recopyings appeared quite surprising. But a few years later, having begun to work for the cinema, I understood that this was the lot of every scenarist who wants to see his work on the screen. Much later, remembering his scenarist with great affection and rare warmth, Pudovkin wrote (and this to a degree confirms my old conversation with Zarkhi): 'He was extremely brave and extraordinarily industrious. His capacity for work was supported by his courage, and his courage, perhaps, would not have been so great if he had not been aware of his capacity for working without respite. In the quest for the perfection of his work, Nathan never feared any amount of revision. Courageously he would throw out entire scenes, which had cost long effort. Well-written scenes, unquestionably successful and, taken individually, quite useful but which he felt damaged the integrity of the ensemble by breaking the flow.'

Yes, the work of the scenarist demands implacable efforts. What an obsession these continual corrections are! First the director: 'Yes, not bad, but you see I had imagined this scene a bit different. If we did it like this?' and it is modified. Corrected. How could it be done otherwise? And it must be corrected so as not to spoil what has been done. Artistically valuable changes must be made without losing in the process what one already has. 'Courageously he would throw out entire scenes. . . .' Yes, that happens too.

Then come the corrections of the studio story editor. And again you reject, interpolate, rewrite, reject again. Circumspectly, for fear of letting escape what is most dear and most important, the thing you are really writing about, in all this revision, in all these debates and meetings, in all this jostling around. Never to lose what is your own! What a job it is to be a scenarist!

Zarkhi was put in charge of the cinema dramaturgy course at VGIK – the only school in the world forming scenarists. He created this Scenarists Faculty with Valentin Turkin, who was an astonishing teacher.

Then one day when we met – we saw each other casually from time to time – Zarkhi told me that he was abandoning the cinema in order to devote himself to the theatre. He had in fact written a play *The Street of Joy*, which was played with great success at the Theatre of the Revolution. And I remember – yes, this I recall perfectly – the anger and bitterness and violence with which Zarkhi then spoke of the cinema. But apparently that also is our common lot, as scenarists: we each swear a hundred times to have done with the cinema – and still come back to it despite everything. The same thing happened with Nathan Zarkhi. He returned to the cinema, and began to work with Pudovkin again. Again they wrote together; and they were together in the car when Zarkhi was killed in a road accident.

Admiral Nakhimov (Pudovkin, 1946) and *Lenin in October* (Romm, 1937)

12. Mikhail Ilyitch Romm

The urbane and self-deprecating wit of Romm's reminiscences affords a clue to the highly civilized personality which his films reflect. Born on 24 January 1901, he served with the Red Army from 1918 to 1921. On demobilization he enrolled in the Higher Art and Technical Institute in Moscow, graduating from the sculpture class in 1925. Between 1928 and 1930 he wrote a dozen scenarios. In 1931 he was assistant to Alexander Matcheret on the film *Works and Men*; and three years later directed his first film (and the last Soviet silent film), an adaptation of Maupassant's *Boule de Suif*. In 1937 he directed the first sound film in which Lenin appeared as an acted character, *Lenin in October*, which was followed two years later by *Lenin in 1918*. From 1954 he was artistic director of the Cinema Actors' Theatre Studio. The seven films which he made in the course of the succeeding twenty-two years did not add greatly to his reputation; but *Nine Days of One Year* (1961), a highly personal study of nuclear research, was regarded as one of the most important Soviet films of the 1960s. It was followed in 1965 by *Ordinary Fascism*, a highly intelligent if wilfully distorted assembly of documentary material. Latterly Romm taught at VGIK and was artistic director of Mosfilm Studios. He died in 1971.

Films: *Boule de Suif* (1934), *The Thirteen* (1936), *Lenin in October* (1937), *Lenin in 1918* (1939), *The Dream* (1943), *Matriculate 217* (1945), *The Russian Problem* (1947), *Vladimir Ilyich Lenin* (1949), *Secret Mission* (1950), *Admiral Ushakov* (1953), *The Ships Attack the Fortifications* (1953; continuation of *Admiral Ushakov*), *Murder in Dante Street* (1956), *Nine Days of One Year* (1961), *Ordinary Fascism* (1965).

The Second Generation

Since this book is supposed to be about the origins of Soviet cinema, I ought to make it clear that I belong to what they call 'the second generation'. The first generation was that of Kuleshov, Eisenstein, Pudovkin, Dovzhenko, Protazanov, Vertov. They were the pioneers, and all my seniors. When I made my first film they were already at the peak of their fame. I came into films at the start of the 1930s, while the Soviet cinema had begun almost ten years earlier; so I can judge the first films only as a spectator.

My birth date . . . but that is rather complicated. My father had been deported and my family lived in Siberia, beyond Lake Baikal. I was a Jew, and the nearest rabbi was at Irkutsk, very far from our village. To register my birth entailed a very long journey* and my father put it off from one day to the next. Eventually he did get round to it, but six months had gone by, and he had quite forgotten the date of my birth – he was a very absent-minded man. He entered the date as being 8 February 1901, when in reality I was born earlier, in January – 24 January to be exact. He had made the trip to Irkutsk in company with a friend, an old Social-Democrat who had also just had a son. On the way my father asked him, 'What are you going to call yours?' 'Ilya, of course, in honour of you. What are you calling yours?' My father blushed, embarrassed and, out of simple delicacy, replied, 'Mikhail of

---

* Until 1917 the civil registers were kept by the local representatives of the various religious denominations.

course – in your honour!' Now the point was that for six months they had been calling me Yura, the name which my mother had chosen. My father registered me as Mikhail, but he didn't tell my mother. Two years later we were moved to another place of deportation. Only then, seeing our identity papers, did my mother perceive with horror that her son was called Mikhail. She flatly refused to call me Misha – Misha, she said, was not her little boy, he was a stranger. Finally, after a family council, they invented the name Moura for me. But Moura is a girl's name. Still people got used to it and it stuck to me right up to school. Then, when my school chums discovered that I was called Moura, like a girl, and surnamed Romm* into the bargain, they started to bully me. This was a very formative experience, and after the third year nobody beat me any more – I had learned to defend myself. . . . Thus, I was born in eastern Siberia, but I was registered at Irkutsk, very far from my real birth-place which is in the present Bouriato-Mongolian Republic, on the river Selenga, in a little town which was called, if I remember rightly, Zaigraievo. Of course nothing of this is mentioned on my identity papers.

The Soviet cinema did not yet exist in 1917, or even in 1919. It really began after the end of the Civil War, at the start of NEP. The atmosphere was very confused, very colourful. At that time I was only a boy, a pupil of the Higher Fine Arts Workshops – Vkhuteyin or Vkhutemas. Mayakovski used to come there often; and we would go to visit the Kuleshov Workshop. This school was frequented by all the Leftish artists. We had as our teachers Malevitch, Arkhipov, Rodchenko, Stenberg and Konenkov, whose pupil I was. This old man – he must be ninety now – has a remarkable memory: he never forgets a face. One evening in 1924 we were at his house – there was Essenin and Isadora Duncan and a crowd of people which included a young man whom no one knew and who was drinking an immense amount of cognac, in common with everyone else in the room. Soon after Konenkov went abroad. When he came back he was an old man.† On his return I went to his studio with a group of friends, among whom was Toporkov, an actor from the Art Theatre. 'I've met you before,' Konenkov told him. 'That's impossible, Sergei Timofeyevitch,' said Toporkov; 'I've always dreamed of meeting you; and this is the first time.' 'No. Don't you remember going to the home of a sculptor, a peculiar old chap, in 1924?' 'I was quite tight and don't remember a thing about it.' 'You came with Isadora Duncan; and it was to my house!' So Konenkov remembered an unknown youngster, seen for a moment in a crowd of people thirty years before.

That was the atmosphere of the times: Essenin, Isadora Duncan, the restaurants, the bars, NEP. . . . And in the midst of all that the pioneers of Soviet cinema led their revolutionary column. Eisenstein, Pudovkin, Dovzhenko – their work bears the stamp of this epoch: they fought for a

---

* The word 'rom' means rum.

† Born in 1874, Konenkov lived in the United States from 1924 to 1945.

revolutionary art and a progressive art, and all under extremely difficult conditions.

When we were young the cinema was not yet an art. It was a curious and not very respectable branch of activity. It was not considered that a decent and capable young man could seriously devote himself to the career of cinema. That is why, later, we came to the cinema by chance, and most often by way of neighbour arts. We suffered failures as actors, sculptors or painters, and we looked for a way out in the cinema. Hundreds of failures of all kinds were thrown into it at the time. It was not difficult to become an assistant, even a director in Moscow or Leningrad. In the Ukraine or in Georgia it was even easier.

The major part of this motley crew of directors was eliminated after the first or second film – some having given proof of outstanding incompetence, the rest becoming simply disillusioned with the work which turned out on trial to be quite difficult. Some stuck to it and became professionals of dubious quality. Others, fewer, proved to be authentic film-makers. So our groups were formed. And, come to think of it, it is by no means the worst way of forming groups.

At that time my contemporaries and myself, representatives of the second generation, had not much to do with the cinema. Gerassimov was an actor making his start under the direction of Kozintsev and Trauberg. Arnshtam was a musician. Pyriev was an actor in Meyerhold's theatre. Raizman only became an assistant director later. Yutkevitch was a theatre designer. Incidentally it is amusing that Eisenstein was a painter at the time when Elisseyev, the *Krokodil* caricaturist, was a theatre director, and Eisenstein designed the sets for his front-line productions during the Civil War. Then, when Eisenstein made *Alexander Nevsky* and I made *Lenin in October*, Elisseyev designed the costumes for both of our films. That is the way we used to change profession! . . .

So, I was a failure. The idea of going into the cinema came to me rather late. I was twenty-eight when I earned my first payment for a scenario for a children's short which I had written in collaboration with three other people. Until then I had practised all the arts except for ballet and the trombone.

By training I was a sculptor. I abandoned sculpture partly because I couldn't find a suitable studio, and to house a ton of wet clay in a bedroom, between the linen and the crockery was as complicated as it was disagreeable. But the principal reason for my giving it up was something else: faced with the clay or the wood I experienced only coldness and boredom; further, quite simply, I just did not believe in my sculpture. I was complimented on it, but I saw quite clearly that other people had more talent than I had. In art mediocrity is useless and detestable.

For the same reason I likewise abandoned literature which, all the same, I had begun to practise seriously.

I was no good for an actor. Theatre direction wouldn't do.

Frustrated, eager and full of joy, I tirelessly sought a real vocation. My different artistic activities did not feed me – I consoled myself by thinking of my disinterestedness. I lived by tracing diagrams, by making translations from French and by typical Vkhutinist odd jobs – arranging exhibitions, decorating the streets for the festivals; I coloured posters and designed book covers. As the proverb says, 'It is the wolf's legs which feed him.'

In 1928 I decided to try my luck in the cinema. After some thought I chose rather an original method of studying this art: I enrolled in the Institute of Methods of Extra-Mural Work (yes, there really was such an institute) as an unofficial auxiliary in the Children's Cinema Department. Every day for four hours I studied the reactions of children from seven to nine, faced with films, and at the same time, I was able to handle the film, to look at any film on the cutting-bench and mess about as I wished, cutting, re-editing and so on. I decided to learn the best films by heart, naively thinking that when I knew *how* it was done, I would be capable of doing it myself. I remember having slaved through nine films in this way, among them *The Battleship Potemkin*, *A Woman of Paris*, Ince's *The Coward*. If someone had woken me up in the middle of the night and interrogated me on, say, shot 140 in *The Coward*, I would have replied at once: 'Medium shot, inn; Torrence in the foreground with his right hand raised holding a cigar, turns, smiling; behind, four people do this and this; through the window may be seen that and that; length of shot, two metres fifty.' In this way I busied myself with cinema – maybe in an absurd fashion, but basically what I had done earlier for the other arts. I worked like an ox, twenty-four hours of the day. And I lived as before: diagrams, posters, translations.

After a year of this I felt sufficiently prepared and I tried to write a scenario. Why, of all the jobs in the cinema, did I choose that of scenarist? Simply because I had a scenarist among my connections, I knew how to work up a scenario, and, moreover, my prior literary activities predisposed me to this kind of work.

My first two scenarios were turned down without any explanation. The next three were rejected too, but with comments. Things were evidently going the right way. So I became a scenarist.

But to be frank, I only worked as a scenarist in order to be able to move on to direction. After I had had three or four scripts accepted, I asked to go and work with Matcheret who was then working on *Works and Men*.

The great day arrived. I was going to say farewell to the Institute of Methods of Extra-Mural Work. My boss was a very charming little old lady. Our relations were pastoral, delightful. After listening to me, she remained silent a moment; then she asked me to leave her office and to come back half an hour later for her reply. When I came back, she greeted me standing, her eyes full of tears, and addressed me exactly as one speaks over the coffin of someone deceased: 'Alas, dear Mikhail Ilyitch! You were a young man of purity and full of talent. You have a good heart, and I love you like a son. Now you are going to enter into cinematographic production. A year from now you are going to become a businessman and a shark. . . . Don't argue –

Nakhimov he came to me in the middle of the night. He had thought up a scene, collected the materials, but his scenarist was utterly exhausted; and he asked me to get him out of a spot. He related the scene to me (it took place between the French and the English commandants), he described their respective characters, all the turns of the scene, its dénouement, everything! I said 'So, what more do you need? Sit down, write it and then shoot it!' 'You must write it for me.' 'All right. You shall have it in two hours.' After he had gone, I set down the scene as he had told it to me. When I took it to him in the morning he was thrilled. He at once made the shooting script – he had now a text on which he could lean. It is this incapacity for writing which was Pudovkin's principal handicap after talking pictures came: this new situation demanded that every director must be able to use his pen and, unlike Dovzhenko and Eisenstein, Pudovkin never could. This explains the striking contrast between his early work and his later films in the sound period.

To get back to my own method of working. Every director who begins a film is inspired by some personal idea. At the time of my débuts, I was very influenced by the early work of Jules Romains: *Le Vin blanc de la Villettes*, *Les Copains*, and so on. I had devoured all the *unanimiste* works of Romains and was extremely delighted by this method of describing a crowd as if it were a single individual. I decided to make this the method of my first films. Thus it is that *Boule de Suif* is a film less after Maupassant, who provided the story, than after Jules Romains, who provided the method.

To my eyes the whole group of travellers in the coach is a single, if nine-headed, being, opposed to the other individual which is Boule de Suif. Consequently I did not need to work each character in detail, but simply gave exterior characteristics. If you look at the film again, you will see that they react like a single being. They get angry at the same time, quarrel or rejoice at the same time. This can be observed in each sequence, and it is exactly the method of Jules Romains at this period. Of course I put my own social concept in the film: I wanted to show that the bourgeoisie is identical in all its ranks; that from the democrat Cornude to the Count, all these people form only a single entity. That was my idea, the connecting thread which I traced through the film – to the degree at least of my means which were not yet those of a professional. Thus *Boule de Suif* is a unanimist film.

One more thing: I have often written that I chose *Boule de Suif* by chance. That is not quite true. If I chose a French theme, the 1870s, it is because I very much wanted to put into practice this unanimist method, and it seemed easier to apply it to this particular raw material. I acted perhaps a little lightly, but my decision was based all the same on concrete reasons. Thirty years have passed since then. My ideas have evidently evolved. When, much later, I made *The Dream*, it was to a degree a return to the theme of *Boule de Suif*, but proceeding from fundamentally different positions. *The Dream* is already a study of human destiny, influenced rather by Tolstoy and Balzac.

The Thirteen, my second film, is the Soviet version of the same idea. It concerned a group of Soviet men, all very different, who together formed a single being, this time representing an ideological concept quite different from *Boule de Suif*. But it is still the same unanimist method. Neither in the one film nor the other will you discover individualized characters. It has even happened that I have given the lines of one character to another. When the principal actor of *The Thirteen* fell ill, I abandoned his role and distributed his actions and lines among the others. This did not worry me in the least: what mattered was to stick to this characteristic method of my *mise en scène*.

Only much later did I begin to work on an individualized character, in my film about Lenin. Since then I have continued to deepen the *particular* characteristics of my personages.

To go back to how I came to make *The Thirteen*.

Less than two months after the release of *Boule de Suif*, I was summoned by the then director of cinematography, Boris Shumyatsky. At the same time he sent for the scenarist I. Prut. We neither of us knew what it was about.

'A friend – it doesn't matter who – has seen an American film,' Shumyatsky told us; 'The action takes place in a desert: an American patrol is wiped out in a battle with the natives, but succeeds in doing its duty.* The film is imperialist, hysterical; but there is an idea that we could do something on the same lines about our frontier defences. Would you like to have a shot at it? You will write the scenario together.'

'Can we see the film?' – 'No, it's already been sent back. But that is of no account. What is important is that you need a desert (we have some very good ones), frontier guards, counter-revolutionary pillagers and that almost all of the men are wiped out. Almost all, but not quite. Note that, Comrade Mikhail.'

I left Shumyatsky a little stunned. 'Well, shall we take a chance?' I asked Prut. 'Have you many other offers?' I had no other offer and I kept quiet.

Silently we left the famous cinema building in Maly Gnezdnikovsky where so many directors have known their biggest successes and the most painful blows of fate.† Still in silence we started to walk down the street.

'We must go into the desert here and now,' I said, and Prut stopped short. 'What for? . . .' – 'To see what there is there. . . .'

'The desert's called desert precisely because there is nothing there,' said Prut sagely. 'It is an empty place. . . . Let us rather begin by thinking up the story. How many heroes shall we have?'

'Thirteen,' I joked solemnly.

'Very well! There's something in that: thirteen. . . . It's mysterious, promises you're not sure what. How if we call the film *The Thirteen*? How does that sound?'

The joke is that during shooting the number of characters was reduced by one. There remain only twelve. But we were already used to this title and we did not want to change it. *The Thirteen* sounded so very well, while *The Twelve* . . . no, *The Twelve* did not sing at all! Anyway *The Twelve* already

---

* John Ford's *The Lost Patrol*.   † Headquarters of the Soviet cinema organization.

existed: Blok's great revolutionary poem of that name is universally known. We just hoped that no one would think to count the characters.

We filmed in the desert. We lived there, too. It was very hot. . . . No, the term is not accurate. It was incredible. You could only bear it once in a lifetime. People fell ill, the heat sent them mad, they wrote desperate letters to Moscow. We couldn't send the film to be developed because the emulsion melted as the train crossed the desert. We dug a sort of deep cave in the sand and we kept the film down there on ice. No one in the group had any confidence in me – it was said that *Boule de Suif* had been made by my former assistant. Not only the actors but a good part of the technicians thought that all these sufferings were in vain and that this adventure should come to an end.

Things went so badly that the direction of Mosfilm decided to stop the production. But I had a very good production director, V. Tchaika; his associate Privezentzev was a marvellous being, absolutely devoted to the cause. Five of us got together: Tchaika, Privezentzev, myself and the cameramen Boris Voltchek and Era Savelieva. We discussed, and decided – to conceal the studio's decision from the rest of the outfit and to continue the shooting.

Of course they stopped sending us money. . . . Telegrams demanding the immediate return of the unit to Moscow followed. Tchaika intercepted the telegrams at Ashkhabad and hid them. We kept on shooting.

Finally a representative of the Studio direction arrived from Moscow with a categorical order: stop the film. But he proved to be an intelligent and courageous man: he helped with the shooting, got a taste of the desert, called a meeting, gave us some good advice and returned to Moscow without having executed the orders of the direction.

During this time the unit went under, slowly but surely: some fell ill, others, whether they liked it or not, had to go back to Moscow. There remained only two out of the five cameramen, one assistant out of four, the accountant worked in his hospital bed, several actors and the whole sound crew had gone. But we pushed on with the work despite everything. And, finally, we finished the exteriors.

When I got back to Moscow, my own sister did not recognize me on the station platform: but in the rushes neither heat nor thirst showed. I had thought that that would come of its own accord, but to my great surprise it all looked rather cool on the screen. So the heat and the thirst had to be *acted* by the actors. . . . And we who did not want to do *mise en scène*, who had struggled honestly with the elements! The sequences shot in a temperature that a good cook might consider just right to cook a pie quickly, looked delightfully cool on the screen. We had to bring a lorry of sand to the studio and start again on all the close-ups. . . .

Yes, this is how it all happened. A bit bizarrely, and a bit by hazard and even, sometimes, quite frivolously. That is what it looks like from the outside. A failure ends up becoming a film director. You might say, in recompense for his tenacity and his virtues.

Mikhail Romm

But there is also an interior aspect of the process. Now, there is scope for a very serious and vast theme. An entirely new theme. It is the history of the formation not of the profession, but of the vision of the world, of the artistic faith of the cinéaste in what determines his destiny in the art. A subject much too vast and grave to be gone into here. Also I will content myself with adding one more thing, extremely important in my eyes: while I was a failure, I was accumulating experience, culture and knowledge of life; I was forming my taste and my artistic conceptions. And then, when I became a director, I set myself to dispense all this, to give it out; and for practical purposes I have ceased to accumulate.

And in fact all that I have managed to do in the cinema I owe to my pre-cinematographic past. I owe it to my service in the Red Army, to meetings with the most diverse and the most interesting people; to the military convoys, the cattle trucks, to the roads and lanes of the Russian countryside where I roved about from 1918 to 1921 (sometimes as a soldier of the Red Army, sometimes as a collector of victuals, sometimes as inspector for the Special Commission of the Revolutionary Military Tribunal). I owe it to my innumerable failures in the domain of the arts. It was these failures which taught me the first elements of literary and artistic culture, taught me to know the smell and the taste of real art, taught me to accept nothing at first sight, without having tried it myself first.

Sometimes a heretical thought comes over me: perhaps it was too soon and not too late that I interrupted my life as a failure in art – an interesting, instructive and useful life – to exchange it for a rapid and, seemingly in all points satisfying career as a film director. For how many more years will I retain the capital? Five? Ten? Or am I already spending the remainder of it? It is impossible to know it oneself. Others will tell you. Those who are younger. Those who, today, consider themselves failures.

Glossary of Persons

Agadjanova, Nina Ferdinandovna (1889–). Scenarist. A communist and revolutionary from 1907, her most notable contribution to the cinema was the script *1905*, of which the single episode actually shot became *Potemkin*. Also collaborated on script of *Deserter*.

Aleinikov, Moisei (1885–1964). Producer. Journalist before the Revolution, after 1917 he was one of the founder-organizers of Soviet film production, and first director of Mezhrabpom-Russ.

Altmann, Nathan. Painter. Belonged, with Soudkin and Chagall, to the Paris school. Distinguished as being one of the only five people who turned up when the Revolutionary Government called a meeting of Petrograd writers and artists in 1917. (The others were Meyerhold, Mayakovski, Ivnev and Blok.)

Andreyev, Leonid (1871–1919). Symbolist and decadent writer, of whose taste for the horrific Leo Tolstoy said: 'He says "Booh!" to me; and I'm not frightened by it'. Best known for play *He Who Gets Slapped* (1914).

Annenkov, Yuri Pavlovich (later Georges) (1889–). Designer. Left the USSR in 1924; worked on Murnau's *Faust* and subsequently settled in Paris where he became well known as a film art director (*Mayerling, La Ronde, Madame de . . .*).

Antonov, Alexander Pavlovich (1898–1962). Actor. Worked first with Proletkult Theatre; then in Eisenstein's *Strike* and *Potemkin*. Continued to act in Soviet films until 1957.

Arnshtam, Lev Oscarovitch (1905–). Scenarist and director. Musical director for Meyerhold's theatre, 1924–7. Entered Lenfilm as sound director – *Golden Mountains* (1931). Co-directed *Counterplan* (1932) with Ermler and Yutkevitch, and made début as director in own right with *Girl Friends* (1936). Best known of later films: *Glinka* (1947).

Babel, Isaac (1894–1941). Writer, especially of short stories, marked by harsh realism, black humour, extremely vivid language. Babel was arrested at the time of the purges following the Moscow trials of the later 1930s. Made several attempts to become a scenarist, one of the last being as writer of the revised version of Eisenstein's *Bezhin Meadow*.

Barnet, Boris (1902–1965). Scenarist and director, originally a boxer. Best-known films: *The Girl with the Hat Box* (1927), *The House on Trubnaia Square* (1928) and *Okraina* (1933).

Bartenev, Sergei Ivanovitch (1900–). Director. Entered films in 1928 as assistant director; subsequently co-director, with Gerassimov, of *The Twelve*. Recently has worked in popular science films.

Bauer, Yevgeni (1865–1917). Director and designer. Joined Russian branch of Pathé in 1912, and afterwards worked for firms of Drankov and Khanzhonkov. Before his sudden death in 1917 made more than eighty films, mostly marked by a taste and pictorialism that came from his early art training.

Blok, Alexander (1880–1921). Symbolist poet who later identified himself fervently with the Revolution (*The Twelve*, *The Punishment*).

Brik, Lili. Actress, wife of Osip Brik and close friend of Mayakovski, in whose plays she appeared.

Brik, Osip Maximovitch (1888–1945). Writer, scenarist, theorist. Associated with Mayakovski in editing *Lef*. Wrote *Storm Over Asia*.

Cherkassov-Sergeyev, Nikolai (1884–1944). Actor. Not to be confused with the more famous Nikolai Cherkassov of *Baltic Deputy*, *Alexander Nevski*, *Ivan the Terrible* and *Don Quixote*. Cherkassov-Sergeyev's most important film role was as Suvorov in Pudovkin's film of the same name.

Chuveliov, Ivan Paulovich (1907–1942). Actor. Played in *End of St Petersburg*.

Dikii, Alexei Denisovich (1889–1955). Actor and director. Worked with Moscow Art Theatre; entered films 1919. Best-known film performances, as Admiral Nakhimov, and as Stalin in *The Battle of Stalingrad* (1945).

Donskoi, Mark (1901–). Director and scenarist. After publishing a novel, entered cinema in 1926 as assistant-director in Moscow studios. First film: *In The Big City* (1928). Best known for the *Maxim Gorki* trilogy (1938–40). Later films include *Heart of a Mother* (1967).

Dzigan, Efim Lvovitch (1898–). Director. Assistant director from 1924 and director from 1928. Best film: *We From Kronstadt* (1936).

Ermler, Friedrich Markovitch (1898–1967). Director. Entered films 1924. Work includes *Fragment of an Empire* (1929), *Counterplan* (1932, with Yutkevitch), *The Great Citizen* (1938–9). In later years he made films for television, though his last important work was the film *Before the Judgment of History* in which the ancient politician Shulgin recalled his years as a member of the last Imperial Duma.

Exter, Alexandra (1884–1949). Painter and designer. Originated in Kiev and spent some time in Western Europe before the Revolution; later designed important productions for Tairov and other theatres. Designed sets for Protazanov's *Aelita*. After mid-twenties worked in Western Europe.

Fogel, Vladimir Petrovich (1902–1929). Actor. Began acting career in Kuleshov's studio, appearing in *The Strange Adventures of Mr West in the Land of the Bolsheviks*, *The Death Ray* and Pudovkin's *Chess Fever*. Last film appearance, 1928, in Roshal's *Salamander* (written by Lunacharski and Grebner).

Foregger (Baron Foregger von Greiffenturn). Theatre director and historian, of Russo-German origin.

Frantzisson, B. V. Cameraman; photographed Eisenstein's earliest attempt at film, *Glumov's Diary.*

Gardin, Vladimir Rostislavovich (1877–1965). Actor, scenarist, director. A stage actor from 1898 (with Kommisarjevsky 1904–6), he first worked in the cinema in 1913, and before the Revolution had made a long series of films based on Russian classics. One of the few important pre-Revolutionary directors to throw in their lot with Soviet cinematography, he directed some of the earliest Soviet films. He continued to direct until 1929, and appeared as an actor until 1950.

Grebner, Georgii Edwardovitch (1892–1954). Scenarist. Came to cinema in 1922 after work as a war correspondent. In silent days collaborated with Lunacharski on scenarios of *Marriage of the Bear* and *Salamander.*

Gusev, Victor Mikhailovitch (1909–1944). Poet and scenarist; frequent collaborator of Romm. Wrote song for Dovzhenko's *Aerograd.*

Heifetz, Josif (1905–). Director. Began film activity with Proletkult, directing first film in 1928 (*Song about Metal,* in collaboration with Alexander Zarkhi and others). His films in collaboration with Zarkhi include *Baltic Deputy* and *A Member of the Government.* In later years, working alone, he has proved one of the most sensitive of Soviet directors, with *The Big Family, Lady With the Little Dog* and *In the Town of S.*

Inkidjinov, Valeri (1895–). Actor and director of Mongolian origin. Studied with Meyerhold; entered films in 1929 as leading player of *Storm Over Asia,* which remains his most important role. Emigrating after a single attempt at direction, he has since acted in France, Germany and Italy.

Kapler, Alexei (1904–). Scenarist. Associated with FEKS group from 1920, acting in some of the group's early films. Assistant to Dovzhenko on *Arsenal* (1929); wrote *Lenin in October* (1937) and *Lenin in 1918* (1939).

Kaufman, Mikhail Abramovitch (1897–). Cameraman and director. Brother of Dziga Vertov, with whom he worked for many years.

Khanzhonkov, Alexander (1877–1945). One of the great pioneer Russian producers. Entered films in 1908. Although his pre-Revolutionary films were of vital importance in the creation of the film industry in Russia, the new revolutionary film-makers saw them as symbolizing all that was old, reactionary and detestable.

Khoklova, Alexandra (1897–). Actress. Grand-daughter of the great Russian art collector and connoisseur P. M. Tretyakov. Collaborator and assistant of Kuleshov (whom she married) from 1916 until his death. Of striking appearance and with an equal gift in comedy and pathos (*Dura Lex*) Khoklova was one of the first great Soviet actresses.

Konenkov, Sergei (1874–). Sculptor. Worked in the USA 1924–45.

Lapin, Boris. Scenarist: *Son of Mongolia* (1936), *He was Called Sukho-Bator* (Zarkhi and Heifetz. 1942).

Leonidov, Oleg Leonidovitch (1893–1951). Scenarist, joined Mezhrabpom-Russ in 1926. Films include Kuleshov's *Sasha.*

Lermontov, Mikhail (1814–1841). Russian romantic poet, killed in a duel at the age of twenty-seven. Author of *Maskerad.*

Levitsky, Alexander Andreyevitch (1885–1965). Cameraman. In cinema from 1910, shot some of the most famous pre-Revolutionary films, including Meyerhold's *Portrait of Dorian Gray,* and may be regarded as a founder of the Russian school of cinematography. After the Revolution his work included Kuleshov's *Strange Adventures of Mr West in the Land of the Bolsheviks* and *The Death Ray*. With Tissé one of the creators of Soviet actuality cinema.

Lobachevski, Nikolai (1792–1856). Russian mathematician and creator of non-Euclidian geometry.

Lomonosov, Mikhail (1711–1765). Russian peasant-born scientist, whose name was given to the University of Moscow.

Malevitch, Kasimir (1878–1935). Painter, leader of Suprematist school, which was defined by Eisenstein as 'a compromise between mysticism and mystification'. This considerably underestimates Malevitch's far-reaching contribution to twentieth-century art.

Mardjanov, Konstantin (1872–1933). Actor and theatre director; a founder of the Georgian Republican theatre.

Matcheret, Alexander Benjaminovich (1896–). Director, scenarist, historian and theorist. Author of influential *The Artistic Currents of Soviet Cinema*. Scenarist of *The Earth Thirsts* (1930) and a number of films up to 1949.

Mayakovski, Vladimir (1893–1930). Leading poet of the Revolution and a vital influence in the formative period of Soviet art. A member of the Futurist group before the Revolution, Mayakovski even before 1917 developed a 'de-poetized' poetry aimed for declamation and the mass audience. This *avant-lettre* Socialist Realism made him the natural spokesman of the young revolution. As editor of *Lef*, an active ROSTA propagandist, an indefatigable writer (of poems, plays, scenarios, journalism) and lecturer, he exerted an immense influence upon the entire generation of the twenties. His suicide in 1930, a few days after the première of his brilliant satire on bureaucratic erosion of society, *The Bathhouse*, in many ways marked the end of the heroic period of Soviet art.

Medvedkin, Alexander Ivanovich (1900–). Director and writer. A pupil of Okhlopkov, Medvedkin was put in charge of a propaganda train in 1931–2, and in the process developed a remarkable line of satirical comedy – a cross between folk-tale, Sennett and dada. A little later, in 1935, *Snatchers* further developed his comedy ideas on lines which were not, alas, to be pursued by Soviet cinema.

Meyerhold, Vsevolod Emilievitch (1874–1942). The most controversial and the most brilliant figure in the theatre of his times. Originally an actor with the Moscow Art Theatre he soon broke away in dissatisfaction with Stanislavsky's 'naturalism'. For most of the first four decades of the century, before and after the Revolution, Meyerhold was a one-man avant-garde in the theatre. Shortly before the Revolution he made two films, *The Portrait of Dorian Gray* and *The Strong Man* which had only small distribution in Russia and have now completely vanished, but which made an enormous impression on artists who saw them. Practically all the most important creators of the classic Soviet cinema – Eisenstein, Ekk, Okhlopkov, Yutkevitch, Roshal, Arnshtam, Straukh, Ilinsky, Martinson – at one time or another came under his influence.

Mosjoukin, Ivan (1889–1939). The greatest cinema star of pre-Revolutionary Russia, Mosjoukin, with his pale romantic face ideally suited to Pushkin heroes, emigrated in 1917, enjoyed a tremendous vogue in France; then went on to failure in Hollywood and death in obscurity and poverty in Paris.

Nemirovitch-Danchenko, Vladimir (1858–1943). Co-founder with Stanislavsky of the Moscow Art Theatre, which he continued to direct after Stanislavsky's death.

Nijinska, Bronislava (1891–). Ballerina, teacher and choreographer; sister of Vaslav Nijinski. Returning to Russia from Western Europe at the outbreak of the First World War, she founded a school with Serge Lifar in Kiev; but finally left the Soviet Union in 1921.

Obolensky, Leonid (1902–). Director. Born Prince Obolensky and enrolled in the Imperial Corps of Pages, he ran away from his family to join the Red Army. Later a pupil of Kuleshov and actor, film-maker and teacher at the Cinema Institute. As a soldier in the Second World War he was captured by the Germans and deported to Yugoslavia. Escaping, he was later captured by the Red Army, charged with desertion and sent to forced labour in Siberia. There he promptly created a film unit. Now director of documentary studios at Tcheliabinsk.

Okhlopkov, Nikolai (1900–1967). Actor and director, notably of theatre, but also active in cinema. Worked with Meyerhold, acted in silent films, and directed three films said to be brilliant (*Mitya, The Sold Appetite* and – never publicly shown – *The Street of Enthusiasm*). Okhlopkov continued to act in films, notably in Romm's *Lenin in 1918* and Eisenstein's *Alexander Nevski.*

Ostrovski, Alexander (1823–1886). Russian dramatist whose works tended to satirize the manners of the rich merchant class and so were much in vogue in early Revolutionary days (*The Storm, The Forest*). Eisenstein's first film was a short insert for a production of Ostrovski's *Enough Simplicity in Every Wise Man.*

Ostrovski, Nikolai (1904–1936). Writer. As a blind, paralysed, bedridden hero of the Civil War, he wrote *And the Steel was Tempered*, about his youth and the fighting Young Communists. Meyerhold's last production was an adaptation of this work.

Piotrovski, Adrian (1898–1938). Scholar, literateur and much-liked script editor at Lenfilm studios. Scenarist of *The Devil's Wheel.*

Polonsky,Vitold Alfonsovich (1879–1919). Popular pre-Revolutionary film star. Originally a Maly Theatre actor, his first film role was as Andrei in the 1915 version of *War and Peace, Natasha Rostova.*

Poslavski, Boris (1897–1951). Actor in *Golden Mountains, Counterplan, Peasants.*

Protazanov, Jacob (1881–1945). Director. Entering the cinema in 1909, Protazanov became one of the most distinguished pioneer Russian directors; and in *Father Sergius* made the most memorable of all pre-Revolutionary films. He emigrated after the Revolution, but returned to the USSR in 1923 where he achieved immediate success with *Aelita*, and continued to direct, specializing in comedy, until 1943 (*Nasreddin in Bokhara*).

Punin, Nikolai. Influential 'Leftist' art critic of the twenties and (1918–19) editor of *Isskustvo Kommuni.*

Pyriev, Ivan (1901–1969). Director. Worked as actor in First Proletkult Theatre; from 1925 assistant in cinema. First film as director 1928. In later years he tended to specialize in rather leaden adaptations from Russian classics (*The Idiot, The Brothers Karamazov*).

Rabinovitch, Isaac (1894–). Painter and designer. Worked for most of the great Soviet theatres including the Bolshoi, Moscow Art Theatre, Vakhtangov. In the cinema his designs included collaboration with Exter on *Aelita.*

Radlov, Sergei. Theatre director. Opened his own studio theatre in Leningrad in 1932, though the most famous production of his later years was his *King Lear* at the Moscow Jewish Theatre.

Raikh, Zinaida (died 1940). Actress, wife of Sergei Essenin (the Symbolist poet and later husband of Isadora Duncan); and afterwards of Meyerhold. She was mysteriously murdered in her Moscow flat while Meyerhold was in gaol awaiting execution.

Raizman, Yuli Yakovlevitch (1903–). Director. One of the most gifted and (in the West) neglected of Soviet directors, working in the cinema since 1924, when he became assistant to Protazanov. Principal films: *Katorga* (1928), *The Earth Thirsts* (1919), *The Last Night* (1937), *Mashenka* (1942).

Reisner, Larissa (died early twenties). Writer. First woman political commissar.

Rjeshevski, Alexander Georgievich (1903–1967). Writer much in favour in the early 1930s (Shengelaya's *Twenty-Six Commissars*, Eisenstein's *Bezhin Meadow*). Generally discredited after 1936.

Repin, Ilya (1844–1930). Great nineteenth-century realist painter, celebrated for his genre pictures and portraits (Mussorgski, Tolstoy).

Rodchenko, Alexander (1891–1956). Constructivist painter, designer and photographer. Designed décors for Kuleshov's *The Death Ray* and *The Journalist Girl*.

Room, Abram (1894–). Director. Originally worked in theatre (in 1914 director of Hebrew Theatre in Vilnus; 1923, director of Theatre of Revolution, Moscow), and journalist. In cinema from 1924. Continued directing into the 1950s, but is now generally remembered for *Bed and Sofa* (1927) and *The Ghost that Never Returns* (1930).

Savchenko, Igor Andreyevitch (1906–1950). Ukrainian director (*Bogdan Tchmelnitski, Taras Sevchenko*); writer of first Soviet musical comedy, *Accordion* (1934).

Semyonova, Ludmilla. Actress much favoured by progressive directors in the twenties. Appeared in *SVD, Bed and Sofa, New Babylon, Fragment of an Empire*, etc. After sound films, her appearances were less frequent though she continued to play occasional film roles until 1956.

Shchors, Nikolai (1895–1919). Legendary hero of the Civil War and liberator of the Ukraine, celebrated in Dovzhenko's film biography.

Shengelaya, Nikolai (1901 or 1903–1943). Georgian-born director. Entered cinema as assistant to Zheliabuzhski. His own best works were *Twenty-Six Commissars* (1933) and *In the Black Hills* (1941).

Shklovski, Victor Borisovich (1893–). Writer, scenarist, historian of cinema and literature. Collaborated on many of the most interesting films of the twenties including *Dura Lex, Bed and Sofa, The House on Trubnaya Square*.

Shumyatsky, Boris. Head of Soviet film industry from 1930 to 1937, dismissed when his grandiose plans to step up film production and create a Soviet Hollywood foundered miserably. Apparently both philistine and anti-Semitic, he was generally unpopular in the industry, and the sworn enemy of Eisenstein whose career he effectively and completely thwarted during the years of his power.

Skvortsov, A. Formerly a teacher at VGIK and assistant to Kuleshov; now artistic director at Byelorusfilm Studios.

Stanislavsky, Konstantin (1863–1938). Actor, theatre director and theorist, co-founder and director of Moscow Art Theatre and one of the most significant influences in world theatre.

Stenberg Brothers. Painters and designers of the Constructivist school whose posters and other cinema and theatrical publicity materials pioneered Constructivist typography and design. Best-known posters for *Potemkin* and Kuleshov films.

Stepanova, Varvara (1894–1958). Constructivist painter and designer. Designed layout for various avant-garde publications including *Lef* and publications of Mayakovski. In 1922 designed Meyerhold's celebrated production of *The Death of Tarelkin*.

Straukh, Maxim (1900–). Actor. Assistant to Eisenstein, and an actor in Meyerhold's theatre. Much identified with his interpretations of Lenin in Yutkevitch's films, for many Russians he is now the physical embodiment of Lenin.

Tairov, Alexander Yakovlevitch (1885–1950). Theatre director, actor and theorist. Founder and director of Kamerny Theatre. (Real name: A. J. Kornblit.)

Tchaikowski, B. V. (1888–1924). Originally a theatre director, entered films as director in 1912. After the Revolution he was one of the first Soviet film directors, organizing an experimental centre for cinema.

Tissé, Edward (1897–1961). One of the greatest Soviet cameramen. Spent childhood in Sweden; in 1914 on completion of studies in painting and photography entered cinema. Worked on newsreel and actuality during war and Revolution; and in 1918 turned to feature films. His major importance however lies in his collaboration with Eisenstein, from *Strike* to *Ivan the Terrible*.

Trauberg, Leonid (1902–). Co-founder of FEKS with Yutkevitch and Kozintsev. His best work for the screen was done in collaboration with Kozintsev, including the early FEKS films and later the *Maxim* Trilogy (1935–9).

Tretyakov, Sergei Mikhailovitch (1892–1939). Writer and dramatist. Formed in the Cubist-Futurist period, was a keen disciple and collaborator (on *Lef*, etc.) of Mayakovski. Best-known plays *Gas Masks* (originally staged by Eisenstein 1923–4), *Roar, China!*. Tretyakov also did the adaptation of Ostrovski's *Enough Simplicity in Every Wise Man* for which Eisenstein filmed *Glumov's Diary*.

Turkin, Valentin (1887–1958). Scenarist. Originally a journalist, Turkin wrote a number of films between 1915 and 1937, the best remembered being Barnet's *The Girl With the Hat Box* and Room's *The Ghost that Never Returns*.

Tynianov, Yuri (1894–1942). Novelist and scenarist; collaborated on early FEKS films, *The Overcoat* and *SVD*.

Vakhtangov, Yevgeni Bogrationovitch (1883–1922). Actor, theatre director, founder of the theatre which bears his name. A pupil of Stanislavsky, was given charge of the Third Moscow Art Studio, where he more and more broke away from the naturalism of the Art Theatre.

Vassiliev, Georgii Nikolaevitch (1899–1940).
Vassiliev, Sergei (1900–1959).
Directors.
Worked together as 'The Vassiliev Brothers' (they were unrelated, in fact), their most memorable work being *Chapayev* (1934).

Vesnin, Alexander Constantinovitch (1883–1959). Painter and designer. First worked as theatre designer in 1917. In 1923 designed Tairov's production of *The Man Who Was Thursday* at the Kamerny Theatre.

Voltchek, Boris Israelevitch (1905–). Cameraman and director. Generally worked with Romm; made his début as director in 1964. Teacher at VGIK.

Zarkhi, Alexander Grigorievitch (1908–). Director and scenarist, entered cinema 1929. The best work of his long collaboration with Josef Heifitz was *Baltic Deputy* (1936).

Zarkhi, Nathan Abramovitch (1900–1935). Scenarist, known especially for his collaborations with Pudovkin (*Mother*, *End of St Petersburg*). Died in car crash in which Pudovkin was seriously injured.

Zheliabuzhski, Yuri Andreyevitch (1888–1965). Director and writer. Entered films as editor in 1915. After Revolution filmed actualities and worked on Soviet pioneer films, the best of them being *Polikushka* (1922). As late as 1946–7 was still working in documentary films and teaching at VGIK.

Index